Hiking
the Endless
Mountains

Hiking
the Endless
Mountains

Exploring the Wilderness of
Northeastern Pennsylvania

Jeff Mitchell

STACKPOLE
BOOKS

Printed in the United States of America

10 9 8 7 6 5 4 3

First Edition

Cover design by Caroline Stover

Cover photo: Hikers Steve Davis and Ashley Lenig at Bradford Falls.
Photo by the author.

All persons facilitating the hikes in this guide do so at their own risk. This
guide is not a substitute for using common sense and caution and taking
the necessary safety precautions. The author and publisher disclaim any
and all liability for conditions along the trails and routes of the included
hikes, occurrences along them, and changes in the data, conditions, and
information contained herein.

Library of Congress Cataloging-in-Publication Data

Mitchell, Jeff, 1974–
    Hiking the endless mountains : exploring the wilderness of
  northeastern Pennsylvania / Jeff Mitchell.–1st ed.
        p.   cm.
    Includes bibliographical references.
    ISBN 0-8117-2648-7 (pbk.)
    1. Hiking–Pennsylvania–Guidebooks.   2. Trails–Pennsylvania–
Guidebooks.   3. Pennsylvania–Guidebooks.   I. Title.
GV199.42.P4 M58   2003
796.51'09748–dc21
                                                            2002011396
    ISBN 978-0-8117-2648-1

Contents

Preface	ix
Introduction	1
State Game Lands 299	9
1. Faulkner Brook	10
Susquehanna County	13
2. Florence Shelly Preserve	14
3. Great Bend (SGL 35)	16
4. Salt Spring State Park	18
5. Woodbourne Forest and Wildlife Sanctuary	20
Lackawanna State Park and Merli Sarnoski Park	23
6. Lakeshore and Kennedy Creek Trails	24
7. Snowflake and Frost Hollow Trails	25
8. Abington and Turkey Hill Trails	26
9. Merli Sarnoski Park	28
Wyoming County	31
10. Keystone College	32
11. The Rocks and Swinging Bridge Trail	34
12. High Knob Trail (SGL 57)	38
Ricketts Glen State Park	41
13. Falls Trail	44
14. Ganoga View Trail	47
15. Evergreen Trail	48
16. Old Bulldozer Road Trail	49
17. Grand View	51

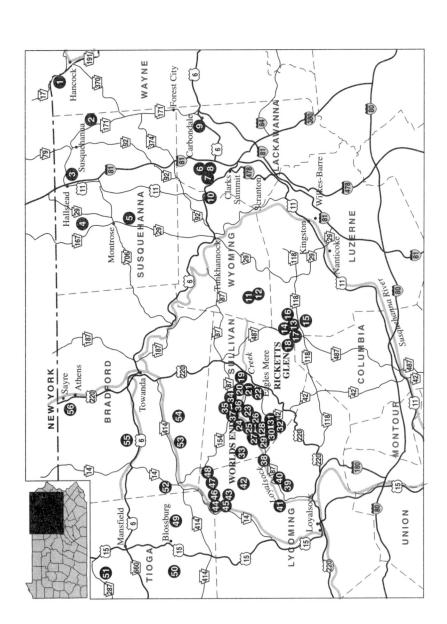

State Game Lands 13   53

18. Twin, Lewis, and Sullivan Falls   54

Wyoming State Forest   61

19. The Haystacks and Dutchman Falls   62
20. Link Trail and Flat Rock   65
21. Pole Bridge Trail   66
22. Shanerburg Run and Rusty Falls   68
23. Double Run Trail and Mineral Spring Falls   70
24. Scar Run   73
25. Ketchum Run Gorge   75
26. Fern Rock Nature Trail   79
27. High Knob Overlook   80
28. Dutter's Run and Ryan's Trail   83
29. Stony Run Trail   86
30. Angel Falls and Kettle Creek Gorge   88
31. Hunters Lake (Pennsylvania Fish and Boat Commission)   92
32. Laurel Ridge Trail   94
33. Middle Branch Trail   96

Worlds End State Park   99

34. Butternut Trail   101
35. High Rock Trail and Alpine Falls   103
36. Canyon Vista   106
37. Worlds End Vista and Cottonwood Falls   109

Tiadaghton State Forest
(Eastern Section)   113

38. Sandy Bottom   114
39. Allegheny Ridge   116
40. Smiths Knob and Painter Run   118
41. Rider Park   120
42. Sharp Top Vista   122
43. Sullivan Mountain   124
44. Miners Run and Band Rock Vista   127
45. Rock Run   129
46. Hounds Run   134
47. Yellow Dog Run and Rock Run   135
48. Sand Spring Trail (Devil's Elbow Natural Area)   137

**Tioga County and State Forest
(Eastern Section)**   139

   49. Fall Brook Falls   140
   50. Sand Run Falls   141
   51. C. Lynn Keller Trail   143

Bradford County   147

   52. Lambs Vista   148
   53. Sunfish Pond County Park   149
   54. Falls Creek   150
   55. Mount Pisgah State and County Parks   155
   56. Round Top Park   158

Hiking Clubs and Organizations   161
Bibliography   163

Preface

I began hiking about seven years ago. It was a chilly March day when I decided to visit a place I had heard about but had never actually experienced—Ricketts Glen State Park. I was utterly amazed by the beauty of this park, but I was disappointed that it had taken me so long to visit and appreciate a place as beautiful as Ricketts Glen. I knew that there were other natural wonders out there for me to see—and so my passion for hiking began.

The only potential problem with having your first hike at Ricketts Glen is that your expectations are immediately raised. But this was not a concern when I visited Worlds End State Park several months later; rather, the very reason I had begun hiking was galvanized.

After hiking Worlds End and the Wyoming State Forest several more times, the outstanding beauty of the region became even more apparent. Here, the natural wonders were not limited to specific areas; rather, the whole region was a natural wonder. I discovered that this area was a wonderland of waterfalls, overlooks, rock formations, white water, and gorges. Few hikers knew about these attributes, probably because some of these places are isolated, the area is sparsely populated, and other regions, such as the Poconos or the Pine Creek Gorge, attract more attention.

Unfortunately, there were no hiking guides that gave in-depth attention to this region, so I decided to write a guide of my own. I soon realized that there were notable trails outside of Sullivan County, and I decided to include hikes from surrounding counties, state forests, and state game lands. As I continued to explore, I expanded the scope of this guide to the Endless Mountains. I felt that the beauty of this entire region needed to be revealed not only to hikers from across the state and nation but also to people like myself, who were born and raised in the Endless Mountains.

I sincerely hope that you enjoy this guide and all the places the trails herein will take you.

I dedicate this book to my niece and nephew Kaitlyn and Christian, Joe, Tessa, Mom and Dad, the rest of my family, and my friends. I give special thanks to Erica Dymond, Steve Davis, Ashley Lenig, Jeff Sensenig, Carissa Longo (don't forget the flashlight), Bob Holliday, Lou Walters, Matt LaRusso, Ian Strever, the Dymond and Reilly families, and Ruth Rode. Thanks to my editors at Stackpole Books, Kyle Weaver and Amy Cooper. Thanks also to the Keystone Trails Association and the Alpine Club of Williamsport for all their work and passion.

At least 20 percent of the proceeds I receive from the sale of this guide will be donated to any or all of the following organizations on a per annum basis: Keystone Trails Association, Alpine Club of Williamsport, Nature Conservancy—Pennsylvania chapter, Northcentral Pennsylvania Conservancy, or other similar Pennsylvania organizations. Please support these worthwhile organizations.

Introduction

Many people think that Pennsylvania's natural wonders are generally located in four areas: the Poconos, the Laurel Highlands and southern Alleghenies, the Pine Creek Gorge region, and the Allegheny National Forest. Undoubtedly, these areas are exceptionally beautiful, but the splendors of Pennsylvania are not limited to these places. Outdoor lovers have long known of the natural beauty that exists in the Endless Mountains and around the Loyalsock, one of the state's most scenic creeks. However, this region's wonders have generally escaped the attention of the public.

"Endless Mountains" is the popular name given to Bradford, Sullivan, Susquehanna, and Wyoming Counties in northeast Pennsylvania. Unlike the Poconos, Alleghenies, and Appalachians, the name Endless Mountains is not geologic. The Endless Mountains are generally considered to be part of the Allegheny Plateau and the Appalachian Mountains.

The Endless Mountains are composed primarily of two distinct geologic, physiographic sections—the Allegheny Glaciated High Plateau and the Allegheny Glaciated Low Plateau. The High Plateau stretches from Potter County in the northwest to Luzerne and Wyoming Counties in the southeast. It is made up of flat, elongated uplands separated from the lowlands by a well-defined, steep escarpment. The High Plateau is capped with highly resistant sandstone and conglomerate and typically ranges in elevation from 1,800 to 2,400 feet. Like most plateaus, the High Plateau is characterized by flat tops with steep mountainsides. It has been heavily eroded by the Tioga River and the Loyalsock, Muncy, Schrader, Mehoopany, and Bowman Creeks, creating numerous gorges, canyons, glens, and white-water rapids. Many of these creeks have tributaries with beautiful waterfalls. This region contains the most spectacular scenery in the Endless Mountains and is the locale of most of the hikes in this guide.

The Low Plateau contains lower elevations with isolated mountains. This region has smooth rolling hills, numerous farms and orchards, and many glacial lakes and swamps. The Low Plateau extends from Tioga to Wayne Counties and south to Pike County. Ironically, the highest peak in the Endless Mountains is in the Low Plateau, at the summit of the North Knob of Elk Mountain, with an elevation of 2,693 feet.

Another prominent geologic feature in the Endless Mountains, located in southern Sullivan County, is the Allegheny Front (also known as the Allegheny Ridge). The Allegheny Front is a mountain ridge that marks the boundary between the Allegheny Plateau and the ridge and valley region. This front is a majestic sight as it rises from the surrounding farmlands to some of the highest elevations in northeastern and central Pennsylvania, reaching 2,593 feet at the summit of North Mountain.

Susquehanna River

To many people, the Susquehanna River is as much a part of the Endless Mountains as the mountains are. The Susquehanna flows past farmlands, towns, and villages and through narrow wooded valleys, taking no shortcuts to Chesapeake Bay. At 444 miles, it is considered the longest unnavigable river in North America. In many places, scenic mountains rise above the river. With its gentle rapids, the river is ideal for canoeing and fishing. The Susquehanna often flows beneath towering cliffs, such as at Wyalusing; the vista from Wyalusing Rocks is famous. There are even some oxbow loops, the most spectacular one being at Vosburg. Unlike the Delaware or the Lehigh, don't be surprised if you have this large, beautiful river all to yourself.

Like most Pennsylvania rivers, the Susquehanna was once accompanied by a canal—the North Branch Canal. This canal connected the Wyoming Valley to Elmira, New York. It was completed in 1855 but did not prove profitable due to maintenance problems, the Susquehanna's predilection for flooding, and the rise of the railroad. Today, there is little evidence of the canal along the river.

Loyalsock Creek

The Loyalsock is one of the most beautiful creeks in Pennsylvania. It is famous among white-water kayak and canoe enthusiasts for its rapids and incredible scenery. It is also a noted trout stream. The name Loyalsock is from the Indian phrase *Lawi-saquick*, meaning "middle creek," because it flows between Lycoming and Muncy Creeks.

The Loyalsock rises in western Wyoming County and quickly enters Sullivan County. By the time it crosses under US 220, the Loyalsock is a sizable stream. At this point, the creek begins to make its greatest cut into the surrounding plateau. The Loyalsock's white water is located primarily between US 220 and Forksville, where there are class III and IV rapids. At Worlds End, the Loyalsock has carved a precipitous 800-foot, S-shaped canyon into the plateau. Many tributaries cascade into the Loyalsock at Worlds End. At Forksville, the creek flows under a covered bridge, one of the most impressive in the state, and joins the Little Loyalsock, its largest tributary. From Forksville to Hillsgrove, the Loyalsock contains some class I–II rapids as it flows through scenic farmlands and abuts steep mountainsides. A mile north of Hillsgrove, the Loyalsock flows underneath another beautiful covered bridge. From this point to the Lycoming County boundary, the creek resembles a small river as it flows through a scenic valley with mild rapids. When it crosses into Lycoming County, the valley narrows, and the Loyalsock is surrounded by sheer mountainsides and rocky bluffs. In some places, the mountains rise almost 1,200 feet above the creek. The Loyalsock then cuts through the Allegheny Front and flows placidly through farmlands until it empties into the West Branch of the Susquehanna River near Williamsport, marking the end of its 60-mile journey.

Trails in this Guide

The trails in this guide are all day hikes varying in difficulty and duration. (The values given for the duration and elevation change of hikes are approximations.) Many of the hikes are not covered by other guides. Personally, I enjoy trails with real scenic value, and these are the types I have included. To appeal to more experienced hikers, some hikes are off-trail or exploratory in nature. Other hikes use trails that are well marked and relatively easy, thus appealing to beginners. Some hikes in this guide may cross private property; please respect all posted signs and the rights of the property owners.

Many of the hikes in this guide use portions of the Old Loggers Path and the Loyalsock Trail, two of Pennsylvania's premier backpacking trails. They also use other hiking trails, jeep roads, old railroad grades, and forest roads. Due to the sizable tracts of public land and the numerous hiking trails, many of the hikes are located in Sullivan County and the eastern section of the Tiadaghton State Forest in Lycoming County. Hikes from other areas in the Endless Mountains are also included.

Keep in mind that the Endless Mountains area is rugged and rocky; thus, almost all the hikes in this guide have the same characteristics. Care and a reasonable degree of physical fitness are required, and hiking boots are usually necessary.

Several hikes in this guide do not follow established trails. It is important that you be comfortable bushwhacking and have the appropriate map when hiking these areas. Some hikes follow streams without the aid of a trail. These hikes tend to be the most difficult, with rugged, slippery terrain and the greatest natural hazards. Care and caution are required.

Loyalsock Trail and the Red X Trails

The 60-mile Loyalsock Trail (LT) is one of Pennsylvania's most famous hiking trails. It was first established by an Explorer Boy Scout post from Williamsport in the early 1950s. In 1953, the Alpine Club of Williamsport was organized to maintain the original 30 miles of the trail. In the early 1960s, the trail was extended to its present length. There have been several relocations since then. The LT, like most Pennsylvania backpacking trails, is maintained by volunteers.

The LT has incredible scenery as it passes waterfalls, vistas, rock formations, and gorges. It explores the Allegheny Front and the surrounding plateau. Currently, there are no shelters along the LT.

While hiking the LT, you will notice several trails blazed with red X's (RX trails). These are connector trails that begin and end at the LT. There are a total of 11 of these trails along the entire length of the LT. Only one of these RX trails has a proper name—the Link Trail. The Link Trail connects Worlds End to Loyalsock Creek 2 miles downstream from the Haystacks, near the Horseheads Iron Bridge. Together, the Link and the LT make for a scenic backpacking loop. Don't confuse this Link with the Link Trail in south-central Pennsylvania. The Scout Loop, a former RX trail, is no longer open for public use.

Contact information: Alpine Club of Williamsport, PO Box 501, Williamsport, PA 17703; website: www.angelfire.com/pa2/alpineclub; e-mail: alpineclub@usa.net

Old Loggers Path

The Old Loggers Path (OLP) is a 28-mile loop in northeast Lycoming County. This scenic trail crosses numerous mountain streams and passes by waterfalls and spectacular vistas. It utilizes several old railroad grades and logging roads dating from decades ago when the area was mined and logged. There are ghost towns in the area, such as Masten, through which the OLP passes. The OLP, which is considered one of Pennsylvania's undiscovered hiking gems, is increasing in popularity. But you can still find plenty of isolation along this beautiful trail. The trail is maintained by the Tiadaghton State Forest and volunteers.

Contact information: Tiadaghton State Forest, 423 East Central Avenue, South Williamsport, PA 17702; phone: 570-327-3450; website: www.dcnr. state.pa.us/forestry; e-mail: fd12@state.pa.us

---

Maps

Individual maps of each hike are included throughout this guide. Below is a legend for the specific features found on the maps.

Map Legend			
	Waterfalls, cascades, rapids, flume, chute	V	View, vista, overlook
	Creeks, streams, runs, brooks		House, cabin, other structure
	Swamps, wetlands		Roads (dotted line indicates extremely rough road)
P	Parking area		Utility, power-line, pipeline swath
	Trail	o—o	Gate
	Other trail		Pool, plunge pool, swimming hole
	Blowdowns, thick brush along trail		Rock slide, talus slope
	Cliffs, ledges, rock faces, boulders	)(	Bridge

The majority of the hikes in this guide can be found on state forest and park maps, which are free to the public. State game land maps cost only a few dollars and can be downloaded from the Internet at www.pgc.state.pa.us. Virtually all the roads that access these hikes, some of which are isolated, are also located on these maps. To help you locate these trails, and as a safety measure, I suggest that you acquire maps of all the state parks, game lands, and forests covered in this guide. The Alpine Club of Williamsport also publishes quality guides and maps of the Loyalsock Trail at a fair price.

Trail Maintenance

The vast majority of Pennsylvania trails are maintained by volunteers, not the government. This is how it should be—trails should be sustained by the people who use them; it is unrealistic to expect state agencies to maintain these trails for us. Many beautiful trails throughout the state forests are disappearing, however. State parks and forests are always looking for volunteers, and trail organizations such as the Keystone Trails Association do an extensive amount of trail work. Many people find that they enjoy the camaraderie of trail work more than they do hiking. Your assistance would be greatly appreciated.

Hiking Safety

It never ceases to amaze me how many people go hiking without taking even minimal precautions to ensure their safety. The Endless Mountains may not be the Amazon or the Congo, but safety precautions are still necessary. Please do the following:

- Bring enough water. Water is absolutely critical, regardless of the difficulty or length of the hike.
- Tell someone where you will be hiking, and if you can, bring a friend.
- Wear proper footwear and dress appropriately for the weather and elevation.
- Bring a snack.
- Bring a map.
- Bring a flashlight and a small medical pack.
- Check the weather report.
- Be careful when hiking along or crossing streams and creeks in high water.

Hiking is an inherently risky activity with changing conditions and numerous natural and man-made hazards. Care, caution, and common sense are required to hike safely. This guide covers hikes ranging from easy to extremely difficult. Please choose hikes that are appropriate for your ability. Many hikes in this guide have dangerous natural conditions demanding respect and experience.

Hiking Etiquette

Unfortunately, some people have no respect for nature. Please note the following:

- Pack out everything you brought in; if you can, pack out litter left by others.
- Do not pick any vegetation or disturb, harm, or feed any wildlife.
- Do not take shortcuts, particularly through switchbacks, which causes erosion.
- Do not deface, remove, carve into, or damage anything.
- Follow all rules and regulations established by the state parks, forests, game lands, or other controlling authority.
- Do not trespass.

State Game Lands 299

State Game Lands (SGL) 299 covers about 2,670 acres in the northeast corner of Pennsylvania. Open hardwoods predominate, but hemlocks and pines can be found along Faulkner Brook and the several ponds. These game lands are stitched with numerous old forest roads and several abandoned quarries. Just south of these state game lands is Hawks Nest, a cliff that provides an excellent view of the West Branch of the Delaware River and its gorge. The area is on private property and not accessible without permission.

Contact information: Pennsylvania Game Commission, Northeast Regional Headquarters, PO Box 220, Dallas, PA 18612-0220; phone: 570-675-1143 or 877-877-9357; website: www.pgc.state.pa.us

1. Faulkner Brook

Duration: 2 hours

Distance: 3.8 miles

Difficulty: Moderate—relatively gentle trail, unblazed; long, gradual ascent and descent

Highlights: Small cascading stream, gorge, scenic mountaintop ponds and wetlands

Elevation change: 500 feet

Directions: From Carbondale, take PA 171 north to the tiny village of East Ararat, where you turn right onto PA 370. Follow PA 370 all the way to PA 191 near the Delaware River. Turn left onto PA 191, heading toward Hancock, New York. Before you cross into New York, make a very sharp left (a fly-fishing shop is off to your right) onto SR 4014. Continue on this road as it follows the river upstream. Near the village of Balls Eddy, SR 4014 bears left; you continue straight on a gravel-macadam road. Follow this road about 1.5 miles into SGL 299. Upon crossing small Faulkner Brook, parking areas are on the left and right.

This hike is located in the northeast corner of the state. The scenic West Branch of the Delaware River is to the east and forms the boundary between New York and Pennsylvania. Follow the unblazed forest road to the left of Faulkner Brook. The trail passes what appears to be an old quarry to the left. To your right, Faulkner Brook babbles over a series of ledges, creating a staircase of small cascades. The trail begins its gradual ascent underneath hemlocks and past boulders. Eventually, the trail moves high above the stream, which is embedded in a deep ravine. The forest continues to be dominated by hemlocks, but as you ascend, hardwoods become more common. Continue the long, gradual ascent as the road passes a switchback of old grades to your left. Soon the trail levels off, and a wetland comes into view off to your right.

Another grade appears from the right, and the road begins another ascent, bearing left and passing another old forest road to your left. Hemlocks continue to cover the deep ravine. The first pond you reach is dotted with old, rotting stumps. This small, isolated pond is a great place to view waterfowl. The trail passes to the left of the pond, along its southern shore.

After making another short ascent, you pass a small pond. When I hiked here in November, a worn dirt path crossed the road and led right into the pond. This path was clear of pine needles, which lay in clumps off to the side as if they had been swept away. I surmised that this was the work of beavers as they dragged sticks and tree limbs down to the pond. You soon reach the gate, a dirt road, and

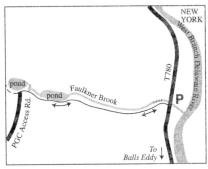

Hike 1: Faulkner Brook

a game land parking area at the second pond. The southern shore of this pond is shaded by a grove of white pines, and its surface is dotted with exposed tree stumps. Like the first pond, this is a great place to view waterfowl or to go fishing. Both these ponds are isolated and scenic. The old forest road continues along the southern shore and wanders off into the woods. From here, return the way you came.

Susquehanna County

Historic and scenic Susquehanna County marks the place where its namesake river first enters Pennsylvania. Unlike the other counties in the Endless Mountains, Susquehanna is dominated not by high plateaus but by rolling hills and mountains dotted with orchards and farms. The entire county was glaciated at one time or another, as evidenced by the many lakes, ponds, and wetlands. Nevertheless, this county is home to the highest mountain in the Endless Mountains, the North Knob of Elk Mountain, rising to 2,693 feet. Although there are no trails leading to the top of Elk Mountain, the ski resort may allow people to occasionally hike the ski trails to the summit in the summer. The views are astonishing as you look over farmlands and Sugarloaf Mountain and Mount Ararat to the northeast. On clear days, the Catskill Mountains can be seen ever farther to the northeast. Susquehanna County lacks extensive public lands, and hiking opportunities are limited; the county is home to about 800 farms totaling about 190,000 acres. However, there are several beautiful places in Susquehanna County worthy of your attention.

🚶🚶 2. Florence Shelly Preserve

Duration:	2 hours

Distance:	2.5 miles

Difficulty: Easy—gradual inclines and declines; rocky trail; wet and brushy in sections

Highlights: Boulders, ledges, swamps, bogs, wildlife

Elevation change: 200 feet

Directions: Proceeding north on Interstate 81 from Clarks Summit and Scranton, exit onto PA 374. Head east on PA 374 toward Lenoxville and the Elk Mountain ski area. PA 374 meets PA 171 at the village of Herrick Center. Turn left onto PA 171, heading north toward Thompson. About 1.3 miles north of Thompson along PA 171, there is a small sign for the preserve and a parking area to your right. It is easy to miss. Stack Road meets PA 171 from the left.

Contact information: Nature Conservancy—Pennsylvania chapter, 1100 East Hector Street, Suite 470, Conshohocken, PA 19428; phone: 610-834-1323 or 800-75-NATURE; website: www.nature.org/wherewework/northamerica/states/pennsylvania

This exceptional 357-acre preserve is owned by the Nature Conservancy. It has a variety of habitats, from rock ledges in open hardwood forests to wetlands, sedges, and bogs. The preserve is home to almost 400 plants and a rare red algae *(batrachorsermum vagum)* that exists only in the purest of water. There are more mammals, birds, insects, and aquatic life here than you can imagine. A diverse forest also calls the preserve home, with a variety of pine and hardwood trees, tamarack, and hemlock.

From the north end of the small parking area, an unblazed trail descends to a narrow country lane at a preserve sign and map. Turn right onto this country lane, which passes in between stone walls, bordering open fields to your left and thick underbrush to your right. The lane gradually descends and arrives at a four-way intersection with a "Thompson Wetland" sign. The trail to your left wanders through a pine forest, passes through stone walls, and eventually diminishes. The lane continues straight ahead and marks your return route. Turn right on the grassy trail as it passes another grassy trail immediately to your left and tunnels through thick underbrush. Before you reach a

wet meadow with springs, make
note of a faint trail to your left
entering the brush and going into
a pine plantation; you will take
this trail on your return.

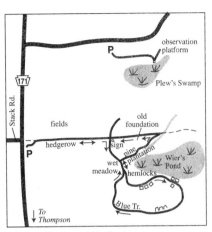

Hike 2: Florence Shelly Preserve

The trail crosses a wet meadow
and enters a grove of hemlocks,
passes boulders, and follows an old
forest road. To your right is the
Blue Trail; you will eventually
return to this point via that trail.
Continue straight as the trail marks
the boundary between hemlocks to
your left and hardwoods to your
right. Turn left upon reaching the
blazes of the appropriately named Blue Trail. The trail passes more
boulders and ledges and soon reaches scenic Wier's Pond, a large glacial wetland encased with sedges and floating bogs. This is an excellent
place to observe wildlife. The trail passes along the shore of the pond
until it makes a sharp right among more large boulders. You now begin
a gradual ascent through a hardwood forest to a series of exposed
ledges and boulders. The trail bears right, passing above ledges and
several boulders. After leveling off, you gradually descend until meeting the trail–old forest road you first hiked. Turn left onto this trail,
where you will cross the wet meadow again.

Now turn right on the trail described previously. This is an unblazed
nature trail. You will have to fight through underbrush before reaching
a pine plantation. The trail enters a field, where you may surprise a few
deer. The trail crosses the lower end of the field and reenters the forest
underneath spruce, hemlock, and pine as it cuts through a small stone
wall. The trail here is somewhat unestablished; just follow the creek to
your right upstream. This creek feeds Wier's Pond. You soon meet the
country lane you first hiked, on which you turn left.

The lane passes meadows, old stone walls, and foundations as it
makes a gentle ascent back to the four-way intersection. Retrace your
steps to your car.

The preserve also has a second, separate trail. This short trail
reaches an observation platform overlooking Plew's Swamp. To reach
this trail, drive about 1 mile north on PA 171 and turn right onto Little
Ireland Road. The parking area is about .25 mile farther on your right.

The trail passes along the boundary between an open field and a hemlock and pine forest. You enter the forest, cross boardwalks, and bear right to the observation platform overlooking Plew's Swamp. This is a large swamp, but it does not contain as much open water as Wier's Pond. Return the way you came.

🥾 3. Great Bend (SGL 35)

Duration:	3 hours
Distance:	6 miles
Difficulty:	Moderate—grassy and gentle; ascents and descents can be long but are typically gradual; trails can be wet and are open, resulting in a lot of sun exposure in summer
Highlights:	Isolation, cascades along small stream, open fields, large wetland
Elevation change:	500 feet
Directions:	From New Milford, proceed north on US 11 toward the New York state line. Upon reaching Hallstead, make a right on Harmony Road (SR 1010), which is before the bridge across the Susquehanna River. Follow Harmony Road for about 2.5 miles to Smokie Hollow Road, which is on your right. Look for the state game lands sign and building. Follow this dirt road for 1 mile until you reach a parking area, where a gated forest road descends from your left.
Contact information:	Pennsylvania Game Commission, Northeast Regional Headquarters, PO Box 220, Dallas, PA 18612-0220; phone: 570-675-1143 or 877-877-9357; website: www.pgc.state.pa.us

Because this loop follows only dirt or grassy forest roads, it is not a particularly beautiful hike. It does, however, offer a pleasant woodland walk with a chance to see wildlife such as deer, wild turkey, and bear. Expect a lot of exposure to the sun if you hike this trail in the summer.

Begin from parking area by hiking up the dirt road, passable to vehicles. You pass an abandoned orchard and pine, hemlock, and tamarack to your right. The road gradually ascends above the small ravine carved by Little Egypt Creek to your right. Hardwoods dominate the forest, with an occasional understory of mountain laurel. After about 2 miles, the road crosses a small wetland fed by the creek and soon reaches a parking area on the right and a gated, grassy road to the left. You may notice three faded blue blazes on a tree near the gate. The blazes do not follow the road.

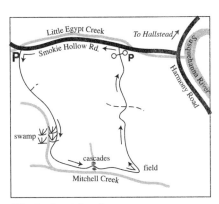

Hike 3: Great Bend

The wide, grassy road begins its winding ascent through glades, meadows, and a young, emerging hardwood forest. At a **Y**, bear left, following the blue blazes. Avoid a logging road to your left with the same blue blazes just ahead. Continue straight on the unblazed road as you begin a long, gradual descent, passing several springs and rivulets. There is a large wetland off to your right. After leveling off, the road continues its winding descent until it makes a sharp left near private property. The trail continues to follow a very wide, grassy old forest road. The scenery becomes a little more interesting where the road curves through a small hemlock-shaded ravine. Here a small tributary cascades down to Mitchell Creek. The road continues its descent until it enters a large field with a few apple trees and partially enclosed by a deer fence. This field offers a partial view of the mountains to the north and east.

Do not cross this field. Instead, make a sharp left and follow another forest road as it ascends the mountain. The road bears left and makes a final climb before reaching a saddle between two mountains. There is a four-way intersection here; continue straight. The road makes a rather steep descent, offering a view to the west, and passes through a pine plantation. Walk around the gate and turn left again to return to your car.

∦∦ 4. Salt Spring State Park

Duration: 2 to 3 hours

Distance: 2 miles

Difficulty: Moderate—hiking along Fall Brook is rocky and slippery and requires you to scramble alongside the waterfalls, so do not attempt it in high water or in winter; trails have moderate ascents and descents

Highlights: Waterfalls, old-growth forest, gorge

Elevation change: 250 feet

Directions: From Montrose, proceed north along PA 29 for about 5 miles until you reach the tiny village of Franklin Forks. You should see a sign for the state park. Turn left on SR 4008 (the only left you can make in this village) and head up Silver Creek, a trout stream. After about a mile, turn left down a dirt road into the park. Drive around the restored farmhouse to the parking area.

Contact information: Salt Spring State Park, c/o Lackawanna State Park, RR #1, Box 320, Dalton, PA 18414-9785; phone: 570-945-3239; website: www.dcnr.state.pa.us/stateparks; e-mail: lackawannasp@state.pa.us

This state park is one of northeastern Pennsylvania's best-kept secrets. While crowds flock to better-known state parks, it is common to have the beautiful refuge of Salt Spring all to yourself. This park offers three scenic waterfalls that tumble through a narrow gorge, an impressive stand of old-growth hemlock, and Salt Spring, of course.

The trails in this park were recently reconfigured, offering numerous hiking options. Two more trails are under development in the western section of the park: Meadow and Silver Creek Trails. Cross the bridge over Fall Brook, and turn right up unblazed Fall Brook Trail, which always stays on the left side of the stream. This wonderful trail is also the most difficult and dangerous. The trail is rocky, slippery, and steep when climbing up the waterfalls; do not attempt it in high water. It follows Fall Brook upstream and climbs alongside all the waterfalls, which are fairly small but scenic nonetheless. The surrounding gorge is rugged and beautiful, with cliffs and rock outcrops. Use caution when negotiating the second waterfall; the trail is eroded and steep and doesn't offer a good foothold. The trail traverses the bank and passes the third and smallest waterfall, which tumbles over a series of ledges. From here, the trail climbs the bank to Hemlock

Trail; it would be difficult to proceed farther upstream because the bank is eroded and steep.

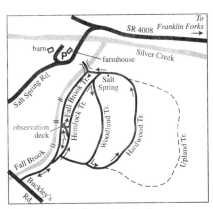

At Hemlock Trail, turn right and descend back to Fall Brook. The trail continues to follow Fall Brook upstream until it meets Buckley's Road. Retrace your steps back to Hemlock Trail. Hemlock Trail is also unblazed and leads you through the park's magnificent stand of old-growth hemlocks. You soon arrive at a boardwalk; turn left and go to the observation platform above the second waterfall. This platform offers a nice view of the falls and the surrounding gorge. Back on the main trail, continue to follow the boardwalk along the rim of the gorge. The trail begins a mild descent and intersects with the blue-blazed Woodland Trail on your right.

Hike 4: Salt Spring State Park

Woodland, Hardwood, and Upland Trails are all half loops. This description follows Woodland and Hardwood Trails, but Upland Trail is also worth hiking. Woodland Trail is mostly level as it takes you through a hardwood forest interspersed with several massive hemlocks. The trail passes one fallen tree that is well over 200 years old. You soon intersect with the yellow-blazed Hardwood Trail to your left. This trail makes a gradual ascent along old stone walls and near the edge of a field that is slowly reverting to forest. Follow the trail as it begins to turn left and passes the red blazes of Upland Trail. Hardwood Trail is mostly level as it follows old forest roads. The trail begins to make a steep descent and turns left on another old forest road, where it is rejoined by Upland Trail. You pass an intersection with Hemlock Trail and soon arrive at the picnic area. Along the way, you pass the park's namesake, Salt Spring. This small spring bubbles out of the ground and has attracted people for centuries, including the Native Americans. In the 1800s, efforts were made to mine the salt, but it wasn't plentiful. From the spring, the bridge and parking area are only a short distance.

Salt Spring is also the locale of a popular legend. During the settlement of Susquehanna County, bands of roving Native Americans periodically attacked the houses of settlers. During one attack, a settler managed to kill several Native Americans but was wounded and taken captive. His wife and children were able to escape. The Native Americans feared pursuit, so they retreated with their captive to a mineral spring and sought shelter in a narrow gorge nearby. They proceeded up the gorge, past several waterfalls, and camped where a small stream flows to meet Fall Brook. Just as they were about to decide their captive's fate, the Native Americans heard the war cry of a band of Oneida Indians. They left the camp to fight their enemy, leaving their captive tied to a tree. During their absence, the wife of the settler, who had followed the Indians up the gorge at a safe distance, arrived to help her husband. But as she untied him, she realized that he had died. In great sorrow, she concealed her husband's body near the spring.

5. Woodbourne Forest and Wildlife Sanctuary

Duration: 1 to 2 hours

Distance: 1 mile

Difficulty: Easy—mild ascents and descents; the trail can be wet, and there may be some blowdowns

Highlights: Swamp, wildlife, old-growth forest

Elevation change: 150 feet

Directions: From Tunkhannock, follow PA 29 north for almost 15 miles until you reach the small village of Dimock. About a mile north of Dimock on PA 29, a sign for the preserve is on your right. The sign and small parking area are very easy to miss. The sanctuary is about 5 miles south of Montrose on PA 29.

Contact information: Nature Conservancy—Pennsylvania chapter, 1100 East Hector Street, Suite 470, Conshohocken, PA 19428; phone: 610-834-1323 or 800-75-NATURE; website: www.nature.org/wherewework/northamerica/states/pennsylvania

About a mile north of Dimock is the Woodbourne Forest, a sylvan gem owned by the Nature Conservancy, which received the property via a donation by Francis R. Cope, Jr. The sanctuary contains a variety of habitats, including open fields, wetlands, and old-growth forest. The trail contains numerous numbered stations indicating points of interest in the sanctuary, so make sure you pick up a guide at the shelter. The biological diversity of this small sanctuary is truly amazing.

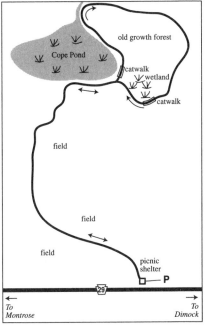

Hike 5: Woodbourne Forest and Wildlife Sanctuary

The trail leaves the parking area and quickly comes upon the R. Gardner Griffin picnic shelter. Here you will find plenty of information about the Nature Conservancy and Woodbourne Forest. Please sign the guest book. Follow the mowed trail as it crosses a field slowly reverting to forest; there are several lilac bushes here. Cross through a hedgerow and an old stone wall and proceed across the edge of another field. The trail soon enters the forest and makes a gradual descent to the swamp, known as Cope Pond.

Cope Pond is a highlight of this hike, as it contains an immense amount of wildlife and 85 species of plants. In the spring and summer, you will be treated to a chorus of frogs and birds. Your feet are bound to get wet, as the trail traverses the edge of the swamp. Here you begin to enter the old-growth section of the forest, dominated by massive hemlocks. Be aware that at stations 22 and 23, the trail turns left and crosses a catwalk over a portion of the swamp. When I hiked here last, it was easy to miss this turn because it was covered with blowdowns. This turn begins the loop through the old-growth section of the sanctuary. The trail continues to stay close to the swamp, offering a wonderful opportunity to view wildlife. You pass a beaver dam to your left after a few hundred feet. Follow the trail downstream, where it turns right on an old forest road. This is the heart of the old-growth forest, and you are surrounded by huge hemlocks. You will notice some trees enclosed in wire fencing to protect them from the beavers.

The trail crosses another catwalk and completes the short loop. From here, simply return the way you came.

Lackawanna State Park and Merli Sarnoski Park

Lackawanna State Park is an ideal place for inexperienced hikers. Its relatively gentle trails explore hardwood forests interspersed with hemlocks and pines, making the trails especially beautiful in the fall. The park's close proximity to the Scranton metropolitan area makes it a popular destination. When hiking here, you will pass by and through numerous stone walls and along the grades of abandoned roads, indicating that these were farmlands that are now reverting to forest. To reach the state park, drive north on PA 407 from Clarks Summit, through Waverly, and into the park, which is less than 3 miles from Waverly. PA 407 passes right through the park. From US 6 and 11 near La Plume, take PA 438 east for about 3 miles. Upon reaching PA 407, turn right into the park. From Interstate 81, exit onto PA 524 and drive 3 miles west to the park.

Contact information: Lackawanna State Park, RR #1, Box 320, Dalton, PA 18414-9785; phone: 570-945-3239; website: www.dcnr.state.pa.us/ stateparks; e-mail: lackawannasp@state.pa.us

Merli Sarnoski Park is operated by Lackawanna County and is located northwest of Carbondale, along PA 106.

Contact information: Merli Sarnoski Park, Lackawanna Parks Department, 200 Adams Avenue, Scranton, PA 18503; phone: 570-876-1714

6. Lakeshore and Kennedy Creek Trails

Duration: 2 hours

Distance: 2 miles

Difficulty: Easy—the trail can be wet and eroded; some mild ascents and descents

Highlights: Lake Lackawanna, forest succession, wildlife

Elevation change: 150 feet

Directions: Heading north on PA 407 from Waverly, turn right onto PA 524, before you cross the bridge over Lackawanna Lake. Pass the park office to your left. Turn left onto Rowlands Road. After about .25 mile, the parking area is on your left.

This pleasant loop is ideal for beginners, children, or those who enjoy trail running. From the parking area along Rowlands Road, follow the light blue–blazed trail as it makes a winding descent to a small brook. The forest is a mixture of hardwood, pine, and hemlock. The trees aren't of substantial size, as this used to be farmland that is slowly reverting to forest. You will also encounter numerous stone walls along this hike. Ascend the other bank of the brook, and you soon come to the dark blue–blazed Lakeshore Trail to the left and the red-blazed Kennedy Creek Trail to the right, which will be your return trail. Follow Lakeshore Trail.

This trail is mostly level, but it can be very wet in spots. Off to your right, notice a plantation of pine trees. The trail bends right above Kennedy Creek, which flows into Lackawanna Lake. If you own a canoe, Kennedy Creek is an ideal place to view wildlife. After making a gradual descent, you approach the lake. The trail follows the shore along an old farm road and offers some nice views out onto the lake through the brush. There is a stone wall directly along the lakeshore.

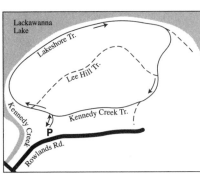

Hike 6: Lakeshore and Kennedy Creek Trails

After about .3 mile, you ascend a bank away from the lakeshore and pass through a small grove of hemlocks and pines. The trail is still level but stays away from the lake. A few hundred feet farther, turn right onto Kennedy Creek Trail, which also follows an old forest road up a gradual ascent through pines and hardwoods. Along the way, you pass what appears to be an abandoned springhouse. The trail continues to climb the hill and passes through more stone walls. Along this section of trail, I startled several deer and wild turkeys. Evidence of farming is all around you: the numerous stone walls, immature forest, the old road on which you are hiking, and open glades that were once fields.

You make a gradual descent, pass near a small stream, and cross over a tributary. You soon return to where you began.

7. Snowflake and Frost Hollow Trails

Duration:	1 hour
Distance:	2.3 miles
Difficulty:	Easy—mild ascents and descents
Highlights:	Diverse forest, Lake Lackawanna
Elevation change:	150 feet

Directions: Proceeding north on PA 407 from Waverly, turn left onto the road accessing the boat mooring and launching area immediately as you enter the park. After about .2 mile, the parking area is on your left. This road continues straight to another parking and picnic area; it ultimately disappears under the lake.

From the parking area, walk pass the rest rooms and behind the boat mooring area. The unblazed trail enters the brush and small trees. Abington Trail, a bridle path, joins from the left, and the trail turns right. Follow the trail as it crosses States Creek and a swamp. The trail ascends the bank, where you reach an important juncture. It is easy to miss the yellow-blazed Snowflake Trail as it leaves from your right and follows the lakeshore. Frost Hollow Trail, your return route, is straight ahead, and Abington Trail comes in from the left. Turn right onto Snowflake Trail. Follow the trail as it tunnels through the thick under-

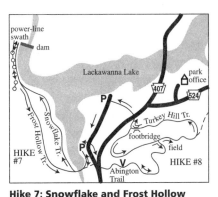

Hike 7: Snowflake and Frost Hollow Trails
Hike 8: Abington and Turkey Hill Trails

brush along the lake. The trail stays close to the lake, but the brush is so thick along the shore that it's hard to get a good view of the lake. After about .25 mile, the trail leaves the shore, crosses a small seasonal stream, and ascends the bank. Here, the forest changes dramatically. It is diverse, with little undergrowth. The forest is dominated by maples, with numerous hemlock, oak, ash, and poplar trees. Some of the trees are sizable. This is an ideal hike in autumn.

The trail rises gradually above the lake along an old woods road, where it meets Frost Hollow Trail, which arrives from the left. Continue straight on Snowflake Trail. The old woods road continues straight ahead, so make sure you follow the trail, which bears right.

The trail is on a steep bank above the lake and passes alongside a power-line swath harboring many wildflowers. This spur trail takes you to a view of the unimpressive dam creating this lake; simply turn around once you reach this point. On your way back to the juncture with Frost Hollow Trail, you may notice an old sign off to your left for "Robin Hood Trail." Because there is no such named trail in the park, it appears to be a sign without a trail. Upon reaching Frost Hollow, turn right onto this trail, which gradually ascends through the forest. As you complete the ascent, you pass small ledges of cross-bedded sandstone and some small boulders. The trail makes a slight descent, crosses a seasonal stream, and passes through and along a few stone walls. You then make a moderately steep descent back to where you started at Snowflake Trail.

8. Abington and Turkey Hill Trails

Duration:	1¹/₂ hours
Distance:	3.2 miles
Difficulty:	Easy—gradual incline along Abington Trail; some mild descents and ascents, but mostly flat

Highlights: Peaceful woodlands, pastoral view

Elevation change: 150 feet

Directions: Proceeding north on PA 407 from Waverly, turn left onto the road accessing the boat mooring and launching area immediately as you enter the park. After about .2 mile, the parking area is on your left. This road continues straight to another parking and picnic area before it disappears under the lake.

From the parking area, follow the access road back to PA 407. Cross the highway and follow Abington Trail. Tunnel through the underbrush as the trail ascends the hillside. Soon the forest opens up, with little undergrowth, and the trail continues its winding ascent. The trail passes through the first of many stone walls stitching this forest. Turn left along another stone wall, then turn right where the trail levels off and passes a pastoral view off to the right. This view is at the top of an abandoned field and overlooks the surrounding countryside. Continue as the trail explores the hardwood forest. Soon you come upon a knoll of ledges. It was here I saw an army of 17 wild turkeys when hiking in early spring. The trail wraps around the knoll, passing near another field, before it makes a quick descent among more exposed ledges. When I hiked here last, there were numerous, randomly placed "No Trespassing" signs on what is clearly state park property. This is the work of unethical hunters who try to keep the public from prime hunting spots.

You soon make another descent, as the trail crosses a field and reenters the forest through another stone wall. You have now reached the loop of Turkey Hill Trail, on which you make a right. This level trail continues until you reach an unmarked juncture in a glade. To the right, Abington Trail leaves to make its descent to Kennedy Creek; to continue on the loop, follow the trail to the left. After about .2 mile, the trail passes some flat, exposed boulders, begins a descent, and crosses a footbridge. A trail leaves from the right; it descends to and crosses PA 407 and arrives at a parking and picnic area along the lake at the end of the access road you first hiked on. If you choose this route, simply turn left at this road to return to your car. Otherwise, follow the remainder of the loop back to the juncture with Abington Trail, over .5 mile farther, where you can return the way you came.

9. Merli Sarnoski Park

Duration: 2 to 3 hours

Distance: 3 miles

Difficulty: Moderate—some inclines and declines; rocky and wet in parts; the trail system can be confusing, with some hiking on trails without blazes

Highlights: Scenic woodlands, ledges, mountain lake, rhododendron

Elevation change: 200 feet

Directions: From Scranton, proceed on US 6 to Carbondale. At Carbondale, turn left onto PA 106 and ascend the mountain along a small stream. Make your first left on Sandy Bank Road. A golf course is on the right side of PA 106. Follow Sandy Bank Road for about .3 mile. The park entrance is on your left. The park road makes a steep climb up to the parking area.

Merli Sarnoski Park covers 844 acres on Fell Mountain and is owned and operated by Lackawanna County. This park offers a pleasant woodland hike that takes you past ledges and around a scenic mountain lake. There are numerous trails here, many of which are unblazed, creating a rather confusing trail system and numerous hiking possibilities. Some of the trails I found myself hiking were ridiculously circuitous. Regardless, Merli Sarnoski Park offers the people of the Lackawanna Valley a scenic sylvan respite. Don't be surprised if you see mountain bikers on these trails.

From the parking area, there's a road near the park office, heading left along the woods. Take this road for a short distance until you reach two short stone walls before the rest rooms. To your right is an unblazed trail through the woods; follow it. You soon reach an intersection with an orange-blazed trail and an unblazed trail, which proceeds straight ahead. This unblazed trail marks your return route. Turn right onto the orange-blazed trail, which wanders through a hardwood forest with occasional hemlocks and pines. The sparse understory comprises mostly brush, saplings, and mountain laurel. The trail bears right across a gravel park road and continues to bear right as it circumvents the soccer fields. Bear left through underbrush and under hemlocks. You then reach an important juncture that is easy to miss—an obvious, unblazed trail continues ahead, but the orange-blazed trail makes a sharp right. Follow the trail right, and you pass a massive oak tree to your left. The trail crosses a spring and begins a moderate, rocky

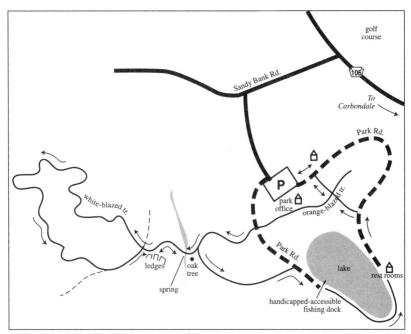

Hike 9: Merli Sarnoski Park

ascent. Pick up an old woods road and bear left through exposed ledges. You soon come to a four-way intersection. To your left and right is the orange-blazed trail, and straight ahead is a white-blazed trail; follow the white-blazed trail. You will eventually return to this spot via the orange-blazed trail to the left.

This white trail is especially circuitous. It ascends and then descends through mountain laurel. You cross another unblazed trail but should continue to follow the white trail. It passes more laurel and begins to wind around the first of many ledges. Because the trail is so curvy, it is important to pay attention to the blazes. The ledges here are low lying and appear to be parallel. At one place, the trail follows the spine of a ledge before making a sharp left turn. The trail descends, curves to the left, and ascends below more ledges and boulders. After the trail levels off, it begins a gradual descent, passing a dilapidated tree fort. You then meet another unblazed trail, on which you bear left. After a few hundred feet, orange blazes appear, and you return to the four-way intersection. Here, make a right, returning the way you came back to the first juncture near the large oak tree, where you turn right, leaving the orange trail.

This gentle, unblazed trail is well established and intersects a park road, on which you turn right and descend to the lake. The road passes a launch and traverses the edge of the lake until it ends at a handicapped-accessible fishing dock. An unblazed, established trail ascends the bank and continues to follow the shoreline through thickets of rhododendron and laurel. This is the most scenic part of the hike. You are offered an occasional view of the lake. The trail passes a few picnic tables and soon reaches the end of the lake at its spillway. When I hiked here one autumn day, there were numerous trout along the shore; the lake had probably been stocked a few days before. Cross the spillway, and pick up a dirt road as you continue around the lake. You pass a beach area and rest rooms. Continue to follow the road. A trail comes in from the left, as does a second a short distance farther. Turn left onto this second trail, which takes you back to where you first met the orange trail. Backtrack to the road and the parking area.

Wyoming County

Wyoming County was named after the Wyoming Valley, which begins in the county's southeast corner near Falls. *Wyoming* is an Indian word meaning "open meadows" or "great plains." Few people know that the Wyoming Valley also gave the state of Wyoming its name. While in Wyoming County, I suggest you stop by Tunkhannock, a revitalized rural community with cafés, shops, restaurants, and numerous Victorian and colonial homes.

Despite its natural beauty, Wyoming County does not have an extensive system of hiking trails. The county lacks a state park or forest, but it is home to extensive state game lands that can be explored by a variety of forest roads, grades, and even a few trails. Some of Wyoming County's beautiful places include the Avery Mountain lookout, spectacular waterfalls and cliffs at Falls, Moneypenny Falls in Eaton Township, the awesome mountain valley at Sugar Hollow, rapids and waterfalls along Meshoppen Creek, Mehoopany Creek and the South Branch of Tunkhannock Creek, Miller Mountain lookout, and the Susquehanna's oxbow loop at Vosburg. Unfortunately, all these places are located on private property and are not generally open to the public. But all hope is not lost. A few trails and destinations in my native county are open to the public and worth exploring.

⣇⣇ 10. Keystone College

Duration:	2 to 3 hours

Distance: 4 miles

Difficulty: Easy to moderate—the trail system is somewhat convoluted; rocky and wet in parts; moderate ascents and descents

Highlights: South Branch of Tunkhannock Creek, wildlife, diverse forest types, cemetery, ravine

Elevation change: 200 feet

Directions: The Keystone College campus is located outside of Factoryville, along Routes 6 and 11, in between Tunkhannock and Clarks Summit. You can turn onto the campus from the highway. From the parking area, walk to the Miller Library, which sits behind Founder's Hall and the admissions office, along the South Branch of Tunkhannock Creek. The trail begins to the left of the library, along the creek.

Contact information: Keystone College, One College Green, La Plume, PA 18440; phone: 570-945-5141; website: www.keystone.edu

These hiking trails are located on the handsome campus of Keystone College. Self-guided interpretive trails and guides are available at Miller Library. The trails are composed primarily of two loops: Nokomis Trail, at 1.5 miles long, and Tunkhannock Trail, at 2.5 miles. Please be advised that there are many side and connector trails, making Keystone College's trail system somewhat convoluted. None of the trails are very long, and they all eventually lead you back to campus, so there is no need to worry, even if you make a wrong turn. Some of the trails appear to be blazed one-way, but they are also clearly established.

From the back of Miller Library, turn onto a grade and make a right onto the swinging bridge, one of two on campus. This bridge really likes to swing, so it's wise not to have too many people cross it at the same time. Below flows the South Branch of Tunkhannock Creek, and this section is special-regulation trout water. Several miles downstream are class II and III rapids. Don't be surprised if you see several kingfishers swoop from tree to tree as they chatter to one another; this is one of the few places in the Endless Mountains I have consistently seen them.

After crossing the bridge, turn right to begin the red-blazed Nokomis Loop. The trail crosses the floodplain of the creek and passes over a small wetland by a bridge. After ascending the bank, turn right. You

soon pass two trails that head off
to the left; continue straight for
now. The trail heads downstream
through hardwoods and stays close
to the creek. Where the creek
makes a sharp turn and flows
toward some rapids, the trail ends,
and you have to turn around. On
your way back, take the first trail
that heads off to what is now your
right. This trail seems to be blazed
one-way but is easy to follow. The

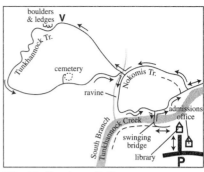

Hike 10: Keystone College

trail makes a gradual ascent through a regenerating hardwood forest
and slowly turns to the left. This section is often wet from seeping
springs. After several hundred feet you arrive at the beginning of a
ravine and Tunkhannock Trail. If you want to take a short hike, turn
left down the ravine and make another left at the bottom; you soon
arrive at the swinging bridge. To hike Tunkhannock Trail, turn right
and cross a small stream.

The trail follows a power-line swath for some distance, passing
springs, brush, small pine trees, and what looks like a Christmas tree
plantation. Follow the trail right onto a narrow dirt road as it begins to
ascend. At the top of the swath you are treated to a nice view of Factoryville and its water tower. The trail turns left, passing through a stone
wall and behind some houses. After making another left onto another
narrow dirt road, you hike by large cross-bedded sandstone boulders.

Continue the gradual ascent into a field offering some more views of
the surrounding countryside. Turn left and follow the trail past some
birdhouses nailed onto orchard trees. The trail then veers right along
the fence of a water catchment basin. Soon you reenter the woods and
descend via several switchbacks and boulders. The trail enters an
open area that will become a forest demonstration project and makes
a sharp left onto another narrow dirt road. Here, the trail is mostly
level and makes a slight descent through abandoned farm fields. If you
wish to see a quaint cemetery, turn left onto the next road and proceed
a few hundred feet. It is guarded by a stone wall, has several old tomb-
stones from the nineteenth century, and is tucked into a forest grove.

Back on the trail, proceed over a small stream and through more
fields and regenerating woodlands. The trail makes a sharp right,
swoops through the forest above a ravine, and soon arrives where you

began. From here, turn right down the ravine described previously. This ravine is one of the highlights of this hike; there are some sizable hemlocks and beech trees, and a small stream tumbles down to the South Branch. At the bottom of the ravine, turn left, passing a bench. The trail stays on the bank and offers some views of the South Branch below. After descending the bank, you arrive back at the swinging bridge.

While you're here, it's worthwhile to explore Keystone College's attractive campus. The college has renovated many colonial and Victorian homes. It's a nice gesture for the college to allow the public's use of these trails.

11. The Rocks and Swinging Bridge Trail

Duration: 1/2 hour; 1 hour for the Swinging Bridge Trail

Distance: 1 mile

Difficulty: Easy to moderate—terrain along Mehoopany Creek is rocky, wet, and slippery; moderate incline and decline along Swinging Bridge Trail; must ford Mehoopany Creek

Highlights: Beautiful flume and pool located in an isolated gorge, ledges and cliffs, Mehoopany Creek

Elevation change: Minimal for the Rocks; 150 feet along Swinging Bridge Trail

Directions: From Mehoopany or Dushore on PA Route 87, turn south on SR 3001 at the small village of Forkston (from Mehoopany, you cross over Mehoopany Creek bridge and turn left). Heading east from Dushore, make a right at Forkston, about 3.75 miles from Lovelton. There are signs for state game lands, and the turn is marked by ball fields and playgrounds along PA 87. Follow this road for almost 6 miles as it follows a beautiful, isolated valley surrounded by steep mountains. After crossing Mehoopany Creek a second time, the road continues for about .5 mile farther. Pay attention where the road turns right underneath hemlocks. There is a small area, with room for two or three cars, to park in on your left. Mehoopany Creek also flows along the road to your left a short distance farther. Park here. You went too far if you cross Stony Brook and begin to ascend the mountain. The Rocks are located on State Game Lands 57.

Contact information: Pennsylvania Game Commission, Northeast Regional Headquarters, PO Box 220, Dallas, PA 18612-0220; phone: 570-675-1143 or 877-877-9357; website: www.pgc.state.pa.us

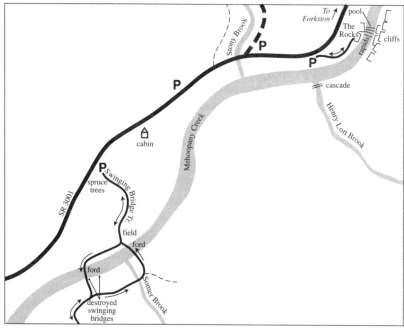

Hike 11: The Rocks and Swinging Bridge Trail

A visit to the Rocks, as the place is known locally, is not really a hike, because it is so close to the road. However, because of its scenery and isolation, it is a worthwhile destination, especially on hot summer days.

From the road, you will notice an unblazed trail heading downstream along Mehoopany Creek. This short trail passes through a grove of hemlocks and reaches the Rocks. Here, the creek has carved a narrow flume through a huge sandstone ledge and tumbles into a large, 12-foot-deep pool. This pool is a prime place to find trout. Although it may be rough on your rear end, it is possible to slide down the flume. The surrounding ledge is wide and ideal for sunbathing. There are several carvings in these ledges. Cliffs rise on the opposite bank. During periods of high water, the Rocks transform into class III+ rapids.

If you walk upstream from the Rocks, Mehoopany Creek has carved an isolated gorge, and its streambed is filled with large boulders and cobblestones. The left bank, heading upstream, is covered with scenic hemlocks. To your left, Henry Lott Brook cascades into the Mehoopany. If you walk up the road from where you parked and turn right on a forest road, you will see Stony Brook. This stream is choked with boulders and cobblestones and has many small cascades. There is another pool where Stony Brook joins the Mehoopany. A short distance up SR 3001, on your right, there is a gated forest road that traverses the side of Stony Brook's gorge. This is a great place to relax and escape from the beaten path.

Swinging Bridge Trail is located about .75 mile farther up SR 3001. From the Rocks, you cross over Stony Brook and begin to ascend. After passing a parking area to your right and a cabin farther ahead on your left, the parking area for the trail is on your left among a grove of spruce trees.

SR 3001 was the setting of one of the most famous murders in Wyoming and Sullivan Counties. A few miles up the road, on March 18, 1892, Jacob Marks, a peddler, was killed by two other peddlers named Harris Blank and Isaac Rosenweig. The two murderers wanted to steal a box of jewelry Marks had in his possession. Blank and Rosenweig had learned of the jewelry while speaking to Marks about their business a month previously. They traced Marks and finally caught up to him on March 18, when Marks was shot twice by Blank. Marks's body was not found until a month later. Meanwhile, Blank and Rosenweig ran off to New York and Milwaukee, before being arrested in Montreal in June 1892. The two were subsequently tried, convicted, and hung in Tunkhannock the following May. On the day of the execution, all the trains entering town were crowded, as were the stores and bars. There were even tickets distributed to allow people to see the double execution, with many people arriving hours early to get a good view.

The trail follows a gated, grassy forest road and is blazed blue. You descend and turn right. Here, you may see faded yellow blazes. These are the blazes of the former Meat Trail, so named because hunters would use the trail, and its swinging bridge, to remove deer they had killed. The Meat Trail crossed Mehoopany Creek and met Southbrook Road and High Knob Trail (Hike No. 12). Unfortunately, this trail has been abandoned and is now overgrown with briers. Parts of this hike follow this former trail. Swinging Bridge Trail continues its descent, passing open fields and glades, which serve as food plots for deer, and reaches Mehoopany Creek. An old forest road continues on the other side and marks your return route. Do not cross the creek; rather, turn right and follow the faded yellow blazes upstream. Along the way, you can see the remains of a swinging bridge. The trail ends at a 2-foot wooden post; here, you must cross Mehoopany Creek. On the other bank, you can see the remains of another swinging bridge. These bridges were probably destroyed by floods because they were too close to the creek along this bank. Cross the creek as best you can, but do not attempt it during periods of high water. Mehoopany Creek is about 30 feet wide and is very scenic with large boulders, cobblestones, small pools, and rapids. You may want to try your luck trout fishing along this isolated stretch.

Scramble up the steep, rocky bank on the other side among a grove of hemlocks. While here, you may want to hike upstream along the bank for a few hundred yards underneath hemlocks. The beauty of this creek continues; it's rare to find a creek of this size with no road, or even a trail, alongside it. Back at the destroyed swinging bridge, follow the faded yellow blazes across another open meadow and through brush and briers. The blazes can be difficult to follow. You soon reach a grassy forest road, on which you turn right. The road bears left and enters a large meadow. When I hiked here one January, I spotted a large porcupine perched on the tiniest branch of a "scag" (a dead tree that's still standing). I'm sure he didn't appreciate, or expect, my being there. The Meat Trail originally continued along the forest road, up to Southbrook Road, but it is now choked with briers. When I was researching this hike, I hoped that the Meat Trail would reach Southbrook Road, which I wanted to use as a partial loop with High Knob Trail. The road accessing High Knob Trail is open only during hunting season, and I was trying to find a suitable year-round access. However, because the Meat Trail is in such bad shape, this wasn't possible.

Backtrack along the forest road; do not return via the yellow blazes. You cross scenic Somer Brook and pass another forest road to your right. This region contains many grades and old forest roads, creating numerous hiking options. You soon return to Mehoopany Creek, which you must cross again. From here, return to your car the way you came.

12. High Knob Trail (SGL 57)

Duration: 4 hours

Distance: 6 miles

Difficulty: Moderate—little elevation change; faded and infrequent blazes; massive blowdowns, thick brush, unestablished trail in sections; very isolated hiking

Highlights: Scenic spruce forests, wetlands, caprock cliffs and boulders, Stone Cabin

Elevation change: 100 feet

Directions: From Tunkhannock, proceed south on PA 29 to Noxen. At the T in Noxen, PA 29 heads left; make a right turn. The road crosses over Bowman Creek, where you turn left. Stay on this road for almost 5 miles. Upon entering the state game lands, keep an eye out where Cider Run Road, a narrow dirt road, ascends to the right; this turn is very easy to miss. Cider Run Road is gated and is open only during hunting season. Do not follow the old railroad grade to the left. This grade eventually leads to Ricketts Glen State Park and is a popular bike path. This grade once transported ice and lumber from Mountain Springs (see Hike No. 16). Cider Run Road is narrow and rocky as you ascend the plateau but is passable by car. Upon reaching the top of the plateau, a distance of almost 3 miles, park at the game lands parking lot to the left. You will see a sign for High Knob Trail.

Contact information: Pennsylvania Game Commission, Northeast Regional Headquarters, PO Box 220, Dallas, PA 18612-0220; phone: 570-675-1143 or 877-877-9357; website: www.pgc.state.pa.us

D on't confuse this trail with High Knob Overlook in Sullivan County. This isolated loop explores the High Plateau and intersects several old forest roads and grades, creating numerous hiking opportunities. In the winter, this would be an excellent place for cross-country skiing and snowshoeing if the trailhead were more accessible. Unfortunately, the trailhead is along a road that is open only during hunting season.

From the parking area, follow the yellow-blazed trail into the forest. Like most plateaus, the forest here is dominated by open hardwoods, with an understory of laurel, brush, and saplings. The trail begins a mild descent and passes a few hemlocks. If you are hiking this trail in winter, look to your left; you may see an interesting rock face on the far side of Cider Run's glen. You begin to follow the remains of a railroad grade. There are still many ties within the grade. The trail is level as it passes over a small stream and through a grove of hemlocks and pines. As you wrap around the southern end of the loop, you pass through increasingly rocky terrain. The trail bears left and meets Opossum Brook Road, a gated forest road. The trail crosses the road and reenters the forest, but if you walk along this road to your left for a few hundred yards, you will see wetlands through which Opossum Brook flows.

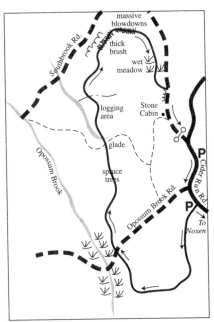

Hike 12: High Knob Trail

The blazes become more infrequent and less established as the trail tunnels underneath spruce and pine. You continue to follow the old, eroded railroad grade. You pass through the trail's greatest asset—a forest of spruce that is unusually deep, dark, beautiful, and green. The trail leaves this sylvan spectacle all too soon, and you again find yourself among open hardwoods. The old grade on which you are hiking eventually enters a meadow, with a grassy forest road joining from the left.

Now comes the bad news: You begin to hike the northern half of this loop. The northern end of this trail is absolutely impenetrable, with immense blowdowns and very thick brush and briers. I have never encountered a trail in such desperate shape. Although I have never hiked any of these alternative routes, you can turn left onto the grassy forest road, which eventually intersects Southbrook Road, on which you turn right. This road makes a long half loop and eventually passes the Stone Cabin. This route, if feasible, would add greatly to your hike.

Otherwise, continue straight and cross a small stream. The blazes are infrequent. High Knob Trail leaves the grassy road and turns left, passing through an open area of ferns. It may be possible for you to continue straight on the grassy forest road, which meets another road and ultimately ends at the Stone Cabin along Southbrook Road. Again,

I have never hiked this route, so if you do, please have the appropriate state game land map.

On High Knob Trail, you soon enter a logged area, and the trail follows a logging road. There are yellow, red, and blue blazes. Regardless of the color, continue to follow the logging road. The road ends, the yellow blazes reappear, and the trail finally enters the woods. The blazes through this section are somewhat infrequent. You hike along a small stream to your right and make a slight descent to a grove of hemlocks. Here, the trail bears right, crosses the small stream, and picks up an old forest road through hardwoods. The trail follows this old, eroded forest road all the way to Southbrook Road. You eventually reach the northern end of this loop. First, the trail passes along a clearcut that has become invaded with dense saplings and brush. The good news is that if you go off the trail and hike a few hundred feet to the left, to the edge of the plateau, there are impressive caprock cliffs and massive boulders. In winter, there is even a partial view of the Mehoopany Creek gorge.

Once you break free of this thick brush, you are treated to blowdowns of gargantuan proportions. For some distance, large trees litter the trail. Blazes are few and far between, but it is possible to follow the old forest road. The blowdowns dissipate as you hike around the northern end of the loop, passing some boulders and more hemlocks. Blazes continue to be infrequent and faded. The trail crosses a wet meadow and descends past ledges and boulders. You soon meet Southbrook Road, on which you turn right.

Hike up gated Southbrook Road as it ascends the eastern side of Somer Brook's glen. There are large boulders to your right. Although I have not hiked all of Southbrook Road, it appears to be in good condition and may offer fine hiking or mountain bike riding. Once the road reaches the top of the plateau, the Stone Cabin is to your right. This scenic, well-constructed cabin sits on a grassy lot. I can only assume that it was built by the Civilian Conservation Corps, or it may be an old hunting cabin. The workmanship in this cabin is definitely worth appreciating. Just ahead, a grassy forest road joins from the right. If you took the alternative route described previously, this is where you may have arrived.

Southbrook Road reenters a scenic spruce forest before joining Henry Lott Road, where you turn right. This road passes a few game commission parking areas and soon returns you to your car.

Ricketts Glen State Park

Many people consider Ricketts Glen the most beautiful state park in Pennsylvania. I'm willing to go a step further: Ricketts Glen is one of the most impressive state parks in the nation and is worthy of national recognition. In fact, Ricketts Glen was slated to become a national park, but World War II ended those plans. Someday, perhaps Ricketts Glen will be made a national park—a status it surely deserves.

Ricketts Glen State Park encompasses three deep glens in the shape of a Y that have been carved into the Allegheny Front and Plateau. The glens are Ricketts Glen, Ganoga Glen, and Glen Leigh. Rainfall collects on top of the plateau and descends through the glens, creating more than 30 waterfalls, 22 of which are named. There are countless cascades between 1 and 5 feet in height. In fact, in some places the water is cascading continuously, making it difficult to differentiate the waterfalls. Ricketts Glen is widely considered to have one of the most impressive collections of waterfalls in the eastern United States. This park also has a scenic mountaintop lake, rock formations, vistas, and an old-growth forest. Ricketts Glen will leave you truly impressed.

Geologically, Ricketts Glen is the result of successive glaciations. Before the Ice Age, Lake Leigh was drained by the South Branch of Bowmans Creek. Ganoga Lake and what is now Lake Jean were drained by Big Run. At that time, Kitchen Creek was a small stream that flowed down the face of the Allegheny Front, much as many small streams do today. After each glaciation, the Lake Leigh drainage was sufficiently impounded from the ice to spill over the Allegheny Front and down Kitchen Creek. By the last glaciation, the stream had eroded deep enough to permanently flow down Kitchen Creek. As for Ganoga Lake and Lake Jean, glacial deposition blocked the drainage down Big Run, and the stream had no other choice but to flow down Kitchen Creek. The combination of increased flow and steep gradient resulted in an amazing number of waterfalls.

Like several destinations in this guide, Ricketts Glen has plenty of history. The park is named after Colonel R. Bruce Ricketts, a veteran of the Civil War. On July 2, 1863, at the battle of Gettysburg, Colonel Ricketts defended his artillery battery from being overtaken by the Louisiana Tigers, who fought for the Confederacy. Surprisingly, Ricketts lost only 7 men in the attack, with 23 wounded. Some believe that if Ricketts had lost his artillery battery, the Union army may have been split in two, and Gettysburg could have been lost. Fortunately, we'll never know. There is a monument to Ricketts in the Gettysburg National Cemetery.

Colonel Ricketts was a wealthy land speculator who lived in a mansion in Wilkes-Barre, now a dormitory at Wilkes University. He also had a summer home, named the Stone House, along Ganoga Lake, just a few miles northwest of the park. The waterfalls were discovered in 1865 by two fishermen who descended along Kitchen Creek from the Stone House. From 1889 to 1893, a crew of six men built the trail among the waterfalls. Ricketts named the waterfalls after family members, friends, and associates, as well as using some Indian-derived names.

Colonel Ricketts owned a vast amount of land around what is now the state park. This land was ultimately timbered and supported the logging town of Ricketts, which is now abandoned, like so many other logging towns in the Endless Mountains. The site of Ricketts is along the Sullivan-Wyoming County border, about 2 miles north of the park. Today, PA 487 passes through the site, but there is nothing left of the town. Over the course of his ownership, Ricketts sought to sell off his land, keeping only the glens and Ganoga Lake. When the state pur-

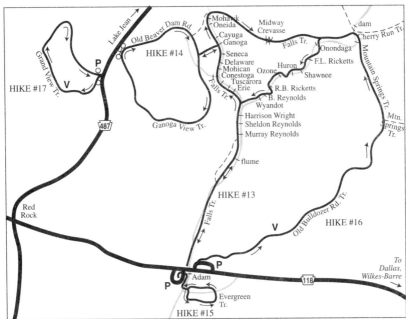

Ricketts Glen State Park
Hike 13: Falls Trail
Hike 14: Ganoga View Trail

Hike 15: Evergreen Trail
Hike 16: Old Bulldozer Road Trail
Hike 17: Grand View

chased the glens, it also tried to buy Ganoga Lake, but its bid was not high enough. Today, Ganoga Lake is owned by a private association. At an elevation of 2,266 feet, it is one of the highest, if not *the* highest, lakes east of the Rocky Mountains.

To reach Ricketts Glen from Dallas, follow PA 415 toward Harveys Lake. Turn left onto PA 118. Follow PA 118 west for about 16 miles, where the highway enters the park and passes the Falls Trail trailhead. From Hughesville, follow PA 118 heading east through Red Rock and into the park. To reach Lake Jean, take PA 487 north from Red Rock. The park is 30 miles north of Bloomsburg on PA 487. The incline up the mountain is steep. You will see a sign for Lake Jean after about 3 miles; the access road is to your right.

Contact information: Ricketts Glen State Park, 695 State Route 487, Benton, PA 17814-7505; phone: 570-477-5675, website: www.dcnr.state.pa.us/ stateparks; e-mail: rickettsglensp@state.pa.us

🏃🏃 13. Falls Trail

Duration: 4 to 5 hours

Distance: 7.6 miles

Difficulty: Difficult—the trail can be steep and eroded and is always slippery; it passes very close to streams and waterfalls, and there are sharp drop-offs near several waterfalls

Highlights: Spectacular waterfalls, rock formations, old-growth forest

Elevation change: 1,000 feet

Directions: It is best to hike the Falls Trail from PA 118. Take PA 118 west from Dallas for about 16 miles. Once you enter the park, there are paved parking areas on both sides of the highway; park in either.

The incredible Falls Trail is the premier trail at Ricketts Glen. This trail takes you past almost every waterfall the park has to offer. Instead of viewing the beauty of the glen from afar, you are surrounded by it. Recently, there has been extensive work along portions of the trail. New bridges have been constructed, and gravel has been laid down over rocky and eroded sections of the trail. Nevertheless, this is still a difficult hike.

The downfall of this splendor is the crowds. On any given weekend with decent weather, the trail is used heavily. I suggest hiking during the week, or even in the rain. I've hiked the glen on several occasions during summer rains when the glens were shrouded in a misty solitude and the waterfalls were even more impressive.

Before you begin the hike into the glen, there is a worthwhile side trip you should take. If you parked in the long parking area north of PA 118, cross PA 118 where Kitchen Creek flows beneath the highway and enter the smaller parking area on the south side of the highway. After passing an old water pump, take the stone steps leading down to the creek. You can soon hear the roar of Adams Falls. Adams Falls is 36 feet tall and has the most interesting erosional features of all the waterfalls. This waterfall has carved itself deeply into the surrounding red Devonian sandstone, creating a thin, powerful stream of water. The falls have also created several "tubs" and a flume before spilling into a deep, clear pool. All the falls below Waters Meet have similar plunge pools. Looking upstream from the top of Adams Falls, you can see that Kitchen Creek has carved an incredibly narrow chasm over which PA 118 crosses. This chasm is no more than 2 or 3 feet wide and hides an unnamed waterfall from view.

Cross PA 118 to begin your hike on Falls Trail. You are immediately surrounded by an old-growth hemlock and white pine forest through which Kitchen Creek flows. The size of some of these trees is impressive; this forest is reminiscent of Cook Forest State Park or the Snyder-Middleswarth Natural Area. Besides the waterfalls, Ricketts Glen's large tract of old-growth forest is its most awesome feature. The trail crosses the creek and eventually crosses back over again. Thereafter the trail splits in two; both paths rejoin at the first waterfall, Murray Reynolds, which is still a half mile away. I usually take the trail to the right, which stays close to the creek. Be aware that blowdowns are common on this trail. The trail follows the creek, rises high on a bank, and then descends to where Kitchen Creek makes a 90-degree bend, creating a beautiful, powerful flume.

The two trails soon meet at Murray Reynolds Falls, a small, 16-foot waterfall with a deep pool at its base. At one time, this waterfall was also known as Pulpit Falls because it is eroding around a pulpit-like rock formation.

The next waterfall is 36-foot Sheldon Reynolds. As you approach Sheldon Reynolds, you can also see the top of Harrison Wright Falls above. During periods of high water, Sheldon Reynolds mimics Harrison Wright as a broad waterfall. During periods of low water, Sheldon Reynolds takes on its more typical hourglass shape.

The trail then makes its approach to Harrison Wright Falls, a broad, even sheet of cascading water. Harrison Wright creates an unusually strong jet of mist that moistens your clothes as you near the falls. This waterfall is probably the most photographed due to its perfect symmetry and the large, deep pool that lies at its base.

The trail then reaches Waters Meet, the heart of Ricketts Glen. It is here that Ganoga Glen and Glen Leigh meet, as do their respective streams. This is an ideal place to rest; you are surrounded by waterfalls as you look up both glens.

Stay on the left and follow Ganoga Glen. Here the trail is steep, slippery, and rocky as it passes Erie and Tuscarora Falls; together, these narrow falls are the second highest in the park. Next is 17-foot Conestoga Falls and countless cataracts and small waterfalls. The trail levels off across rocky terrain and approaches a small tributary with its own waterfall. Cross the tributary on a bridge, and the trail enters my favorite place in Ricketts Glen. Here the trail wraps around ledges and underneath overhanging rocks, right next to the waterfalls. The roar of the falls reverberates against their rocky confines. The state park trail map says that Seneca, Delaware, and Mohican Falls are here, but it is hard to discern which falls are which because they explode from everywhere and are continuous.

The trail then makes its approach to Ganoga Falls, a stunning 94-foot waterfall. A trail leads to the base of the falls. After a heavy rain, this waterfall is deafening. Return to the main trail and climb it past the switchback, where a trail takes you close to the crest of the falls. Do not venture too close to the falls or the cliff; people have been seriously injured at Ganoga Falls. From here, you have no choice but to return to the main trail and follow a switchback to the top of the falls. Along the way, you pass a spur connecting to Ganoga View Trail (Hike No. 14).

From here, the trail levels as it passes Cayuga and Oneida Falls, two of the smallest falls in the park. Here, the hemlock forest is especially aromatic and verdant. Soon the trail makes a steep ascent to Mohawk Falls. It is here that Kitchen Creek spills from the top of the plateau into Ganoga Glen.

The trail crosses a bridge over the creek, and after a few hundred feet, you will see a sign for Highland Trail. Turn right onto Highland Trail. This trail offers a nice respite from the roar of the waterfalls in the glens. Due to the high elevation, the one sound you will hear is the wind as it sweeps across the treetops. The trail crosses a small stream and soon passes through Midway Crevasse, which is composed of massive boulders and rock formations. From here, the trail makes a gradual descent to Glen Leigh, where eight named waterfalls and countless others await you.

Glen Leigh is steeper than Ganoga Glen, and the stream is almost constantly cascading. Here, the trail is very close to the stream; at times, you are almost walking in it. In some places the trail is so close to the waterfalls that you can almost stick your hands in them. The first waterfall is 15-foot Onondaga, a charming waterfall framed by hemlocks. The trail descends closely on the left and then crosses the creek directly above F. L. Ricketts Falls. The trail used to descend very close to the left of this falls, but it had to be rerouted to the other bank due to flooding of the unstable wooden steps. The new route is very well constructed as it descends to the bottom of F. L. Ricketts and crosses the stream again. A short side trail to the left takes you to the foot of the falls.

Next are Shawnee and Huron Falls. Here the trail makes a sharp descent on rock steps alongside these falls. What's most impressive about these falls is that they are carving a massive overhanging cliff of fractured sandstone on the other side of the stream. Numerous springs descend from this cliff.

The portion of the trail to the crest of Ozone Falls is sometimes inundated with water, and you may have to rock hop; cross the bridge at the top of Ozone. The park map says that Ozone is 20 feet high, but it appears much higher. The trail descends to the stream via a switchback.

Next is R. B. Ricketts Falls, with some rock overhangs where you can get a beautiful view of the falls and another delicate waterfall as it descends on the other bank. The trail crosses the stream again and winds around B. Reynolds Falls, then crosses the stream again above Wyandot Falls. At these falls, the stream is constantly cascading, so it's tough the determine where B. Reynolds Falls begins and ends. It is possible to crawl behind some of the falls. From here, the trail soon reaches Waters Meet. From Waters Meet, simply take the trail back to PA 118.

14. Ganoga View Trail

Duration: 2 hours

Distance: 4 miles

Difficulty: Easy—mostly level, with some steep inclines; often wet due to springs; one stream crossing

Highlights: Pleasant woodland hike, broken views of Ganoga Glen, mountain laurel blooms in June

Elevation change: 200 feet

Directions: This description begins from the spur trail above Ganoga Falls. The trail passes near PA 487, just above the start of Grand View Trail (Hike No. 17), on the right of the road, 2.3 miles from PA 118 at Red Rock. It is marked by a gated forest road. Parking is very limited here.

From the top of Ganoga Falls, follow a gentle, grassy spur trail through a mix of hardwoods and hemlocks. To the left is a glen carved by a small stream. After about .3 mile, you reach the white-blazed Ganoga View Trail; turn left onto the trail. Ganoga View is a wide trail that becomes a snowmobile path in winter; mountain bikers also use it. The trail descends and crosses a small stream and enters a forest dominated by hemlocks. Here the trail is on the edge of Ganoga Glen. There are broken views through the trees of both Ganoga Glen and Glen Leigh. The trail is very wet in several spots from springs.

The trail then begins to move away from the side of the glen, and the vegetation is dominated by hardwoods with a thick understory of mountain laurel. In some areas the forest appears sparse, due to either windstorms or insect infestation. The trail gently ascends and crosses the headwaters of Maple Spring Run. It makes another ascent and passes through a glade. Hemlocks reappear as the trail nears Maple Run. The park map shows the trail crossing Maple Run twice, but it never comes close to the run. You can hear cars on PA 487 off to your left. Soon the trail makes a gradual descent into a hemlock grove, makes a somewhat steep ascent over a bank, and levels off. The trail then arrives at a short spur trail to the left that connects to PA 487; there is a log bench here. Ganoga View Trail ends here, but continue by proceeding to your right onto Old Beaver Dam Road, which is blazed yellow. Here the trail makes a gradual descent through the hemlocks and is very wet in several spots. Eventually, the forest opens up to include some glades, and hardwoods become more prevalent. This section of the trail has many wildflowers. It was here that I heard the gurgling of a stream, yet I couldn't see one. Old Beaver Dam Road leads off to the left and goes to the top of Mohican Falls. Go straight where the trail makes a steep, rocky descent back to where you started.

15. Evergreen Trail

Duration:	1/2 hour
Distance:	1 mile
Difficulty:	Easy but somewhat inaccessible; off-trail hiking, bushwhacking
Highlights:	Mature hemlock and white pine forest

Elevation change: 30 feet

Directions: Park in the parking area on the south side of PA 118. The trail begins below Adams Falls.

Although flat and easy, the unblazed Evergreen Trail is inaccessible because there is no bridge across Kitchen Creek, so you have to ford the stream. Furthermore, the bridge that crosses Boston Run has a fallen tree across it. Despite this, Evergreen is a short trail worth hiking, as it is isolated and takes you through an impressive stand of old-growth hemlock and white pine.

Follow the trail downstream from Adams Falls; the trail passes in front of small cliffs and overhangs. After about 100 yards, you'll see Boston Run joining Kitchen Creek on the other bank. Cross Kitchen Creek here, but do not attempt to ford it during periods of high water. Follow the trail on the left side of Boston Run, which is a small stream. The trail crosses Boston Run via a bridge that supports a fallen tree. From here, the trail wanders through a mature hemlock and white pine forest with some very large specimens. The forest is deep and verdant. The trail crosses Boston Run again. Here the trail is not well established; it is best if you head downstream along Boston Run, keeping the run about 100 feet to your left. You soon pick up a faint trail that returns to the run near where the bridge crosses it. Return the way you came.

 ## 16. Old Bulldozer Road Trail

Duration:	4 hours
Distance:	8 miles
Difficulty:	Moderate—the trail begins with a long ascent with one steep section but then levels off; several stream and spring crossings
Highlights:	View, waterfall, breached dam
Elevation change:	1,000 feet
Directions:	The trail begins from the large parking lot on the north side of PA 118.

This trail is linear. To make a scenic loop, hike up Bulldozer Trail and then hike down Glen Leigh and Ricketts Glen back to PA 118. Old Bulldozer Road Trail is blazed red. This description also includes a mile of Mountain Springs Trail.

From the trailhead, the trail passes by a picnic area and through a stand of mature hemlocks and white pines. Here the trail is mostly level, with some gradual ascents. The trail makes a right and begins a long ascent up the rim of Ricketts Glen and enters a forest dominated by oaks and other hardwoods. The trail levels off but soon begins a steep climb. Near the top of this steep climb, you will notice a faint trail off to your left. This very short trail goes to Valley View, which offers a broken vista of Ricketts Glen, Beaver Pond, and the valleys to the southwest. The view is bisected by a large white pine. Here I saw many hawks and turkey vultures off in the distance.

Old Bulldozer Road Trail continues to ascend, curves right among several large rocks, and reaches the top of the mountain. You'll see a trail sign propped up against a tree; its original post is across the trail. The sign states that this is Valley View, but there is no view to be seen. You may see a faint trail off to your right, but it goes nowhere—definitely not to a view.

From this point, the trail is level and begins a slow descent to Mountain Springs Trail and Glen Leigh. The vegetation here is dominated by oaks, laurels, and some evergreens. The trail is wide, grassy, and fairly easy to walk. It also tends to be wet, as there are several springs and a few small stream crossings. After 2 miles, Bulldozer Trail ends and joins Mountain Springs Trail, which is blazed with orange triangles. Make a left onto Mountain Springs and follow it into a hemlock stand up a rocky forest road. There are numerous springs that feed a stream to your right. This stream is Bowmans Creek, which flows for about 40 miles before joining the Susquehanna River near Tunkhannock.

If you turned right onto Mountain Springs Trail, you would reach Mountain Springs Lake after about 2 miles. During the logging era, this lake was known as Ice Dam No. 2, with Ice Dam No. 1 being downstream. These dams were intended to be splash dams to float logs downstream, but they failed to transport lumber effectively. As a result, the dams were used to cut and pack ice. Huge conveyor belts and processing houses were built along the dams. Saws were used to cut the ice off the dammed lakes. The adjoining village of Mountain Springs became dedicated to the production of ice, not lumber. However, with the advent of refrigeration, the need for ice evaporated, and the village met the same fate as neighboring lumber towns. The state subsequently purchased the ice dams. Ice Dam No. 1 was condemned and drained. Ice Dam No. 2 was enlarged to become Mountain Springs Lake, now owned by the Pennsylvania Fish and Boat Commission.

Continue left onto Mountain Springs Trail. The trail passes streams underneath hemlocks and makes a slow curve to arrive at Glen Leigh, with its cascades and a tiered, unnamed 20-foot waterfall. Directly ahead is a breached dam that once held Lake Leigh. Although it is an eyesore, the dam is unique, in that it is "hollow." Most dams are solid blocks of concrete, but this dam has a retaining wall no more than a foot thick that rises diagonally downstream; it is supported with several walls. You can walk underneath this retaining wall. It is hard to imagine that this dam was strong enough to hold back any amount of water; maybe that is why it was breached. Colonel Ricketts supposedly built this dam, as well as another, with the hope of generating hydropower. This investment failed, and the state ultimately condemned and drained the lakes. Ironically, beavers have built their own dam at the breach, creating a small pond.

Turn left on the road, cross the stream, and go up the slight hill. You will soon see a trail to your left that goes down into Glen Leigh. You can either turn back the way you came or complete the loop by taking this trail down into the glen. This trail follows the stream closely and is surrounded by beautiful hemlocks and white pines. Here, the stream is placid and is dammed by fallen logs. Soon the trail meets Highland Trail, which arrives from the right. You can once again hear the waterfalls and cascades of Glen Leigh.

17. Grand View

Duration:	1 hour
Distance:	1.9 miles
Difficulty:	Easy—gradual inclines and declines; rocky and wet in parts
Highlights:	Vista

Elevation change: 100 feet

Directions: From PA 118, turn onto Route 487 at Red Rock, heading north toward the park office, Lake Jean, and a camping area. The road makes a steep ascent up the mountain. It bears left, passes an open quarry, and bears right. A gated forest road on your left marks the beginning of the trail. Parking is limited; do not block the gates. The trailhead is roughly 2.5 miles from Red Rock.

Follow the gated forest road as it ascends to the left. The trail passes through an oak forest with an emerging undergrowth of white pine, hemlock, maple, mountain laurel, and beech. Follow the intermittent blue blazes as the trail continues its gradual ascent and turns right. You hike through a logged area and then reenter the forest. The trail makes a slight descent, then a steeper climb, and you reach the fire tower at Grand View. The area around the tower is open because it has been logged. From one of the highest points in Luzerne County, you have nice views of the Allegheny Front and Ricketts Glen to the east, the Susquehanna Valley and ridges to the south and southwest, and a glimpse over the High Plateau to the west. It is illegal to climb the fire tower. Colonel Ricketts built a 40-foot observation tower at this site, but it has been torn down. It is believed that 3 states and 11 counties can be seen from Grand View.

From the tower, follow the trail, now blazed red, through blueberry bushes and scrub vegetation. The trail soon takes a sharp right, makes a rocky descent, and tunnels through the blueberry bushes. You reenter the forest and pass along a boundary line with private land. The trail is rocky, but not very difficult, as it makes a gradual curve to the right through the forest and ferns.

You then come upon another sign indicating that you should turn right on a wide, grassy trail. Follow this trail as it makes a gradual descent to where you started.

State Game Lands 13

Encompassing almost 50,000 acres, SGL 13 offers a lot of room to explore. Like in most state game lands, there are numerous old forest roads and grades here. The western part of SGL 13 is dominated by the deep gorge carved by scenic West Branch Fishing Creek in between the plateau and the Allegheny Front. North Mountain rises above the source of West Branch Fishing Creek. The top of the plateau holds many ponds, swamps, and other wetlands. These ponds and wetlands are then drained by streams that cascade down the side of the plateau. A perfect demonstration of this can be found in the eastern section of SGL 13, where Heberly Run, Sullivan Branch, and their tributaries have carved steep, rugged glens into the plateau. These glens hold numerous waterfalls and cascades. This unique area is as beautiful as it is rugged. If you love waterfalls, have an adventurous spirit, and have grown tired of the crowds that plague Ricketts Glen, this is the place for you.

Contact information: Pennsylvania Game Commission, Northeast Regional Headquarters, PO Box 220, Dallas, PA 18612-0220; phone: 570-675-1143 or 877-877-9357; website: www.pgc.state.pa.us

18. Twin, Lewis, and Sullivan Falls

Duration: 5 to 8 hours, depending on the routes taken

Distance: 8 miles

Difficulty: Difficult to extremely difficult. If you stay on the forest roads instead of hiking up and down the streams, this hike can be classified as difficult. If you choose to hike up and down the streams, this is an extremely difficult hike with several dangerous sections. The hike up Heberly Run is not as taxing as the descent of Sullivan Branch. Hiking along the streams is very difficult, as the terrain is slippery, rocky, wet, and steep in sections. There are no trails following the streams, so you must be comfortable scrambling, bushwhacking, and traversing steep, rugged ground with loose footing. The descent along Sullivan Branch is extremely difficult due to the large number of waterfalls, which are often surrounded by cliffs and sheer ledges. There are countless stream crossings, and you may often be hiking in the streams themselves. This hike is probably the most difficult in this guide. I strongly suggest that you carry a Pennsylvania Game Commission or topographic map.

Whether you hike the forest roads or along the streams themselves, you must cross over the top of the plateau, which presents a different set of challenges. You must be comfortable hiking in isolated areas of dense brush with faded, inconsistent blazes and numerous blowdowns.

You must be an experienced, fit hiker to tackle this "trail." Take every safety precaution, and hike when there is plenty of daylight. High water and ice make it impossible to explore these waterfalls.

Highlights: Waterfalls, cascades, flumes, chutes, chasms, pools, cliffs, ledges, and erosional features; several isolated, steep, rugged gorges and glens

Elevation change: 1,200 feet

Directions: Proceeding west along PA 118 from Red Rock, turn right at a sign for Jamison City and Central Park Hotel after about 4.5 miles. Follow this road to Central. After passing the hotel, make a right to Jamison City. Both villages are located in a scenic valley surrounded by towering mountains. Travel through Jamison City (really a village) and into the state game lands. Once you pass through Jamison City, keep an eye out to your left for a towering brick chimney hidden in the forest. Stop at the large parking area along Sullivan Branch. The parking area is about a mile from Jamison City. (Jamison City was named after B. K. Jamison, a wealthy Philadelphia banker who was a business associate of Colonel R. Bruce Ricketts. Jamison financed a railroad that extracted lumber from Colonel Ricketts's property; this railroad passed through Jamison City. It was common for land and lumber barons to name towns after themselves.) Central is 20 miles east of Hughsville on PA 118.

Almost everyone knows about Ricketts Glen and its waterfall wonderland. However, very few people know about the waterfall wonderland just west of Ricketts Glen, in State Game Lands 13. This is because these waterfalls are isolated, and most of them are hard to reach.

This hike begins with choices. If you want to follow the easier route, which bypasses the vast majority of waterfalls and cascades, hike up Grassy Hollow Road through a grove of hemlocks. The gate between the parking area and East Branch Fishing Creek marks your return. Grassy Hollow Road is generally open to vehicles during hunting season but gated the rest of the year. The road begins its gradual climb and offers some limited views of the towering plateau. East Branch Fishing Creek and Heberly Run are out of sight but can be heard. All three major waterfalls along Heberly Run can be heard from the road. After roughly .5 mile, you should be able to hear a waterfall in the glen; this is Big Falls. Another .5 mile farther is Twin Falls; the upper

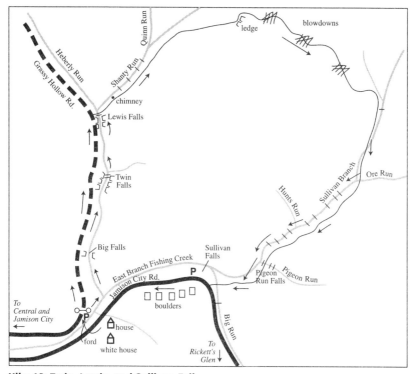

Hike 18: Twin, Lewis, and Sullivan Falls

falls of Twin Falls can be seen from the road as it shoots through a small chasm. About .5 mile farther, there is a small, grassy parking area on your right with a sign for Lewis Falls. Turn right onto a narrow, old forest road, and you soon reach the top of Lewis Falls. Lewis Falls is about 30 feet high and drops into a deep plunge pool. It is very difficult to reach the bottom of this waterfall because it is surrounded by cliffs and overhanging ledges. Above the falls, Heberly Run slides over smooth sandstone. Shanty Run joins Heberly Run just upstream from the falls, with its staircase of small cascades.

A hike up Sullivan Branch and Heberly Run is very difficult, but it gives you the full experience of this beautiful glen. There is no trail. Heading upstream, East Branch Fishing Creek babbles over a cobblestone streambed with an occasional boulder and ledge. The terrain is generally more level on the right bank of the stream. After about .5 mile, Heberly Run arrives from the left; follow it. You soon enter the glen of this stream, and the terrain becomes much more rugged. Boulders, ledges, and cascades dominate the stream. A cliff rises on the right bank, and Big Falls comes into view soon thereafter. Hemlocks dominate the left bank. Big Falls is about 25 feet high and has a beautiful plunge pool. It is totally surrounded by cliffs and overhanging ledges. Two rivulets cascade from the left.

To bypass Big Falls, you have to scramble up the steep bank on the left. The terrain, especially above the falls and pool, is very rugged, with sudden drops. Above the falls, the stream has carved a series of flumes, chutes, and pools into the bedrock. Heberly Run bears to the left over another flume as more rivulets cascade down the left bank. The scenery and erosional features in the streambed are superb. After bearing right, there are more beautiful chutes, cascades, and a few boulders. Ledges rise on both banks. The stream babbles over cobblestones underneath more overhanging ledges, which become more pronounced as you move upstream. You soon reach the lower falls of Twin Falls, a 10-foot falls emptying into a pool. Scramble up the ledges to your right. Above the lower falls are the upper falls and its churning whirlpool. The uppers falls can be seen from Grassy Hollow Road.

Continuing upstream, there is another waterfall of a tributary off to your right. Cobblestones dominate the streambed almost all the way to Lewis Falls. You know you are nearing Lewis Falls when overhanging ledges and cliffs begin to rise on both banks, a typical feature of this stream. Beautiful Lewis Falls soon comes into view as it tumbles into a pool against a ledge. Cliffs and ledges surround the falls. To reach the top of the falls, go to a place 100 to 200 feet downstream on the right bank (east) where the ledge has been sufficiently eroded so that you can scramble up. It is a steep climb with loose footing.

Once you reach the top of the falls, you are at the same place you would be if you hiked up Grassy Hollow Road. From here, bear right onto an old forest road or grade as it follows Shanty Run upstream. The grade is unblazed and passes boulders. Ledges can be seen farther up the mountainside. The grade passes to the right of an old chimney of some sort, a remnant of the logging era. The grade can be choked with brush at times, but it is generally distinguishable. As the grade climbs the plateau, waterfalls and cascades can be seen and heard below. Shanty Run moves out of view as the grade continues to ascend. You come to a place where one grade bears left and follows the run, and the trail follows a grade to the right. The grade to the left can be taken for a short distance to more cascades. I've been told that farther upstream, Shanty Run and Quinn Run join each other amidst waterfalls.

As you near the top of the plateau, the drop to Shanty Run is precipitous as the grade passes underneath hemlocks. Once you reach the top, the fun really begins. The grade completely disintegrates as it becomes choked with brush and saplings; however, a trail is somewhat noticeable. As is typical of plateau forests, the forest canopy is sparse, and the underbrush is thick. Fortunately, small blazed dots help guide your way. These blazes come in an assortment of colors, including fluorescent orange, red, and pink. They can be hard to follow at times. The trail passes a spring as it traverses the plateau and reaches a crumbling ledge capped with a scenic grove of hemlocks. Make a hard left here and follow the trail as it curves to the right through the hemlocks. There is a broken view of the plateau from the ledge.

You then reach a very confusing juncture as you enter an open area of ferns surrounded by blowdowns. The trail makes a left as it traverses the blowdowns. The blazes can be hard to follow, but they're there. The trail becomes easier to follow as you pass through an open hardwood forest. It makes a wide semicircle to your right to avoid another blowdown area. You then begin a slight descent, and there is yet another blowdown. The trail goes straight through it. The most confusing parts of this trail are when it meets blowdowns, but don't panic; there is a way around them.

The trail meets a small stream off to your left and begins to descend to your right, where it picks up another old forest grade or road. The blazes disappear. To your left is Sullivan Branch, and the trail soon passes a waterfall that is hidden from view but can be clearly heard. This waterfall drops over an overhanging ledge and is about 20 feet high. The grade continues to descend to the right of Sullivan Branch. The grade crosses the stream but is nonexistent on the left bank of Sullivan Branch; simply head downstream. The grade gradually reappears as you pass cascades. Another grade descends from the left and joins the trail before crossing Ore Run. From here, the grade is more established, but blowdowns may pose a problem. Sullivan Branch is completely out of view, and this route avoids the numerous waterfalls along it. The grade crosses a small stream that cascades downstream before meeting Sullivan Branch. The grade continues its gradual descent, and after about 1.5 miles it crosses Pigeon Run admist a beautiful miniglen. There are waterfalls both upstream and downstream from the grade. Pigeon Run tumbles downstream across bedrock with flumes. The grade descends, and Sullivan Branch can again be seen for a short distance. It enters a glade, crosses Big Run, and meets Jamison City Road (Big Run Road). Upon joining Big Run, Sullivan Branch becomes East Branch Fishing Creek.

If you want to see the waterfalls along Sullivan Branch, you have no choice but to descend along the stream. There are no trails or blazes; you must bushwhack extensively. Although the beauty is incredible, the terrain is very rugged and difficult. Cliffs, ledges, and steep banks make passing around the waterfalls treacherous. The waterfalls and cascades themselves are often located within chasms carved into the bedrock. It almost seems necessary to have canyoneering equipment to traverse parts of Sullivan Branch. The isolation and beauty of this rugged gorge surpass that of Ricketts Glen, but the difficulties and dangers of descending along Sullivan Branch cannot be underestimated.

For approximately .25 mile below Ore Run, Sullivan Branch babbles over a cobblestone streambed with an occasional cascade or pool. The stream passes through an open floodplain dominated by ferns. From here, Sullivan Branch transforms from a benign mountain stream into a waterfall and cascade wonder. The first falls has three tiers and is about 40 feet high. This waterfall is surrounded by cliffs. I was able to descend along an eroded portion of the cliff on the right bank, but this descent is particularly difficult. The stream swirls through chutes before shooting down another waterfall and chasm. Two more waterfalls are immediately downstream. All these waterfalls are encased in cliffs and overhanging ledges. In many places, the stream is encased in long, deep pools carved into solid rock. Because of these features, it is difficult to bypass the numerous waterfalls along their steep, loose, brush-laden banks.

The stream flows through another cascade and into a pool before making a sharp curve over another waterfall. This falls is about 30 to 40 feet high and has a beautiful plunge pool. The surrounding terrain is extremely rugged. Farther downstream, Hunts Run cascades from the left amidst more chutes and flumes. Overhanging ledges and cliffs return as they surround three more waterfalls and cascades. The stream sweeps through several flumes and chutes before dropping over a small cascade into a deep pool—one of many along this stream. Two more cascading waterfalls remain downstream. From here, Sullivan Branch cascades along a large cliff to your right. A short distance farther, Pigeon Run plunges 30 feet almost directly into Sullivan Branch from the left. The scenery is spectacular. This marks the end of the waterfalls, for now. A few hundred feet downstream, you will notice a grade, or old forest road, on the left bank. Follow this grade up to the trail and grade discussed previously.

Once you reach the road, bear right and gradually descend. You will immediately notice a parking area to your right. Follow the short trail from the parking area, and you come upon the highest, largest, and most impressive waterfall of all—Sullivan Falls. Sullivan Falls drops about 40 feet into an awesome pool. Above the falls, a narrow chute has been carved around a ledge. It is difficult to reach the bottom of the falls because the surrounding banks are steep.

Return to the road and follow it 1.5 miles downstream. Large boulders and ledges litter the mountainside to your left. After .75 mile, East Branch Fishing Creek returns in view. As you near the parking area, which is on the other side of East Branch Fishing Creek, you pass a beautiful old farmhouse and an outbuilding. You then have to turn right, ford East Branch Fishing Creek, and pass the gate to the parking area and your car.

Wyoming State Forest

One of Pennsylvania's 20 state forests, Wyoming State Forest encompasses almost 43,000 acres and has 90 miles of hiking trails. It contains some of the most scenic places in Pennsylvania. Mountain biking and horseback riding are also allowed there. A beautiful picnic area is located at Dry Run, which is close to Dry Run Falls.

Contact information: Wyoming State Forest, 274 Arbutus Park Road, Bloomsburg, PA 17815; phone: 570-387-4255; website: www.dcnr.state. pa.us/forestry; e-mail: fd20@state.pa.us

19. The Haystacks and Dutchman Falls

Duration: 2¹/₂ hours

Distance: 4.6 miles

Difficulty: Easy to moderate—some rocky areas; several small stream and spring crossings; moderate inclines and declines

Highlights: Waterfalls, white-water rapids, the Haystacks, railroad grade

Elevation change: 250 feet

Directions: Heading south on US 220 from Dushore, cross over the Loyal-sock Creek and proceed .8 mile, where you make a right onto Mead Road. Proceed on Mead Road for .2 mile; on your right is a large, circular gravel parking lot. The trailhead for Loyalsock Trail (and for this hike) is at the far end of this parking lot. Mead Road is about 3 miles north of Laporte along US 220. Parking is not allowed along US 220.

The Haystacks hike is probably the most popular one in Wyoming State Forest. This hike is accessible, relatively easy, and incredibly beautiful. The land surrounding the Haystacks was first purchased by the Nature Conservancy in 1978 and then transferred to Wyoming State Forest.

Begin at the Loyalsock Trail (LT) trailhead. Here, the trail is steep and rocky. As you descend, the surrounding forest quickly changes from hardwood to hemlock. You soon reach an old railroad grade; much of the return hike will be on this level grade. About 100 feet to your right is Dutchman Run. Follow the stream down to the top of Dutchman Falls, passing a few campsites. Dutchman Falls is about 40 feet high and plummets almost directly into Loyalsock Creek. It is best to view the falls from the top, but if you're feeling adventurous, you can scale the steep and rocky embankment to the bottom. Dutchman Falls was also known as Amber Falls at one time, probably due to the tannin in the stream.

Leaving the falls, you will notice one of the red X (RX) trails. The 11 RX trails are connector trails; they all begin and end at the LT. Here, the RX trail makes its way up to the railroad grade. It passes a couple of springs and is very rocky. However, it is probably best to return to the railroad grade the way you came.

The railroad grade is almost perfectly level and is ideal for biking or hiking with small children. After approximately .5 mile, you will see a red and yellow arrow on your right and a small dirt trail. Keep an eye out for it, because it is easy to miss. Here, the LT leaves the grade. The trail begins a moderate descent to Loyalsock Creek and follows the creek closely. The water is almost mesmerizing with its strong current and clarity. During periods of high water, you may see kayakers on their way to tackle the Haystacks.

Still keeping close to the creek, you will notice that the forest on your side of the creek is dominated by hemlocks, while the other bank is dominated by hardwoods. This is because the southern bank faces north, resulting in the cooler temperatures that hemlocks favor. The northern bank of the creek faces south, resulting in greater exposure to the sun, which hardwoods favor.

The trail temporarily leaves the Loyalsock to cross a tributary but quickly returns to a scene of several rapids. The trail leaves the Loyalsock again, where it follows an old forest road. You cross several springs and a small stream. It was here that I saw a porcupine desperately trying to climb a birch tree as I approached. I almost felt guilty

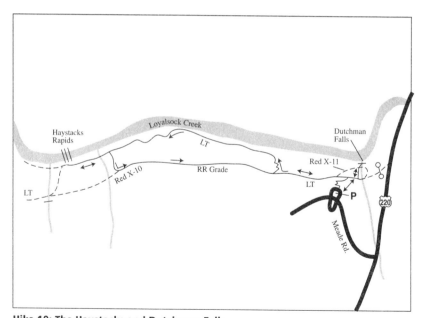

Hike 19: The Haystacks and Dutchman Falls

for disturbing him. The trail returns to the Loyalsock on a bank high above the creek and soon descends to a gravel forest road and crosses a stream. To the left are several campsites. When I hiked here in May, I saw a beautiful bush of brilliant pink star-shaped flowers on the bank. The trail follows the Loyalsock closely and passes more campsites. As you approach the Haystacks, the trail becomes narrow and rocky. Soon the trail levels out and widens to a wonderful camping area that overlooks the Haystacks, which are to your right.

The Haystacks are large boulders of white Burgoon, a highly resistant sandstone. They create class IV–V rapids during periods of high water, with enormous waves. At lower water levels, this is a popular swimming area, with a natural whirlpool in the center of the rapids and two deep pools. Be careful jumping from boulder to boulder, because the surface is smooth and can be slippery. During the logging era, the Haystacks frustrated any attempt to use the Loyalsock as a logging run. As a result, the logging companies made repeated attempts to blast the Haystacks with dynamite. Fortunately, they failed.

If you'd like to see a wet-weather waterfall, follow the LT from the Haystacks. The trail ascends along a small stream and makes a steep, rocky climb to the same railroad grade described previously. There, you can see a delicate waterfall cascading over numerous ledges. From here, you can return via the railroad grade or return to the Haystacks.

The unblazed trail heading downstream along the Loyalsock passes several campsites, crosses a small stream, ascends the bank on the other side, and makes a gradual descent to the Loyalsock. As it nears the Loyalsock, it passes a few more campsites before reaching the rocky shore, passing massive boulders. If you follow the shore downstream a short distance, you will reach a ledge rising about 10 or 12 feet above the creek, where there is a swimming hole about 10 feet deep. This is a great place to jump in the water and go swimming, especially if the Haystacks are crowded.

Upon your return from the Haystacks, follow the trail the way you came until you reach the point where you see blazes for the LT and the RX trail. The LT is the way you hiked in and follows the creek. The RX trail follows a gravel road to the railroad grade and is an easier return. To return via the RX trail, make a right onto the gravel road and follow it up to the railroad grade, where you make a left. Notice that all the trails here have the RX blazes; follow any of these trails, and they all lead you to the LT. The grade is eventually joined by the LT. Return the way you came.

🚶🚶 20. Link Trail and Flat Rock

Duration: 1¹/₂ to 2 hours

Distance: 2.8 miles

Difficulty: Easy to moderate—mostly flat, with short but steep inclines and declines; can be slippery where the trail nears the creek; do not hike this trail during high water

Highlights: Loyalsock Creek, Horseheads Bridge, Flat Rock

Elevation change: 150 feet

Directions: From Worlds End, proceed east along PA 154 for about 2.5 miles until you come to Shanerburg Road on the right. This road is the first right from Worlds End. There are a few parking places along Shanerburg Road. To begin from Horseheads Bridge, follow PA 154 from US 220 at Laporte for about 2 miles and turn right onto Rock Run Road. The bridge and a few parking places are about .75 mile farther.

A lthough Loyalsock Creek is one of the region's prime attractions, few trails explore it for any distance. This trail is the exception as it passes through hemlock groves, crosses ledges along the creek, and traverses banks. This hike can be begun at either Shanerburg Road, where it meets PA 154, or at Rock Run Road at the historic Horseheads Bridge. This description begins at the bridge.

Horseheads Bridge is a beautifully maintained iron bridge built in the late 1800s. The bridge offers nice views both up and down the creek. Don't cross the bridge; rather, proceed downstream, following the red X blazes of Link Trail. Link Trail is a connector to Loyalsock Trail (LT). It offers a more direct route between Worlds End and Horseheads Bridge. With the LT, Link Trail offers a wonderful weekend backpacking trip; I suggest you begin from the Haystacks. This description does not follow the Link in its entirety; rather, it describes the scenic section between the bridge and Shanerburg Road. Thus, you will have to backtrack unless you brought two

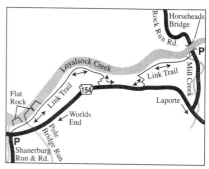

Hike 20: Link Trail and Flat Rock

cars to park at either end. But this trail is so scenic and short that there is no need to do that.

The trail begins by passing through a beautiful hemlock and pine grove at the edge of the Loyalsock; there are several campsites along this section of trail. To your right, the Loyalsock tumbles over small rapids, around boulders, over ledges, and into several deep pools. The creek often flows up against crumbling cliffs. It is wonderful to have this creek all to yourself.

The trail continues along the creek until it makes a sharp left and ascends the bank to PA 154. This reroute was necessary because the trail had been washed out downstream and it was too dangerous to hike along the steep bank. After ascending via switchbacks, the trail arrives at PA 154, which it follows for several hundred feet. Upon reentering the forest, the trail makes a sharp descent, passes under some blowdowns, and soon returns to the creek. The Loyalsock continues its habit of tumbling over rapids and then calming down into deep pools. Soon you arrive at PA 154 and Shanerburg Run. This part of the trail is tricky, because you have to ford the run where it meets the Loyalsock. You may have to scamper up to PA 154. After crossing the run, the trail traverses the edge of several ledges, which are often slippery. These ledges are known locally as Flat Rock and border a pool. This is an ideal place to enjoy the sun or take a swim. A short distance ahead, the Link crosses PA 154 at Shanerburg Road; from there, you have to retrace your steps.

21. Pole Bridge Trail

Duration:	2 hours
Distance:	1.5 miles
Difficulty:	Moderate—expect blowdowns; moderate inclines and declines
Highlights:	Trout streams, cascades, pools, hemlock and other forest types

Elevation change: 350 feet

Directions: From US 220, turn onto PA 154 just north of Laporte. Follow PA 154 into Wyoming State Forest. After about 4 miles, turn left onto Shanerburg Road. Shanerburg Road is the first right along PA 154 heading from Worlds End State Park. Once you turn onto Shanerburg Road, there is a place to park along the right side of the road.

T his hike explores Pole Bridge
Run and its isolated glen. Pole
Bridge Run, like its sister stream to
the west, Shanerburg Run, is a
small, scenic stream harboring sta-
ble populations of brook trout, the
state fish. Because these are small
streams, your fly may spend more
time in the trees and bushes than
in the water.

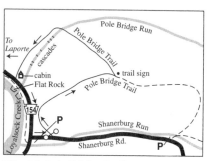

Hike 21: Pole Bridge Trail

Hike up Shanerburg Road and
make a sharp left on a bridle trail
as it ascends along a gated forest road. The trail curves to the right and
climbs the flank of the mountain, passing boulders, ledges, and a scenic, diverse forest of pine, hemlock, and a variety of hardwoods. The
trail soon meets its trail sign, where you turn left. The trail straight
ahead is also known as Pole Bridge Trail and makes a half loop back
down to Shanerburg Run and Road at the beginning of Hike No. 22.
You can extend your hike by taking this trail, but you will have to hike
down Shanerburg Road to reach your car.

Pole Bridge Trail descends rapidly along the side of the glen to its
namesake run. This beautiful, isolated glen is covered with hemlocks.
Numerous blowdowns are a problem along this section. The trail
meets the run and crosses it without the luxury of a bridge, so be careful fording it in high water. This is a scenic spot, as the run flows
through a deep, beautiful forest.

There is some interesting history behind Pole Bridge Run. About 2
miles upstream, where the run flows from Celestial Lake and underneath PA 42 (about 2 miles east of Laporte), was the settlement of
Celestial. One square mile of this land was deeded to "Almighty God
and his heirs in Jesus Messiah." Peter E. Armstrong was the leader of
this religious colony, which he established in 1864 to await the end of
the world. Many homes were built, and the foundation was set for a
massive tabernacle. The colony soon disappeared, however, and the
land was sold at a tax sale a few years later.

Back on the trail, you follow the run for only a few hundred feet
before the trail turns into an old forest road and ascends the other side
of the gorge. The run is dotted with boulders and has many cascades
and pools. The trail levels off high above the run and then descends to
PA 154 as it passes a cabin. Pole Bridge Run is a beautiful stream as it

tumbles down to the Loyalsock via more cascades, flumes, and deep pools. If you're feeling adventurous, you can simply follow the run down to PA 154; it is a much more beautiful but difficult hike.

Once you reach PA 154, simply turn left, and Shanerburg Road is a short distance down the road. Along the way, you pass the Link Trail. The section of the Link along Loyalsock Creek is worth your attention (Hike No. 20).

22. Shanerburg Run and Rusty Falls

Duration: 2 to 3 hours

Distance: 3 miles

Difficulty: Moderate—mild inclines and declines; numerous stream crossings; often wet

Highlights: Shanerburg Run, waterfalls, beautiful forests, open meadows

Elevation change: 300 feet

Directions: From US 220, turn onto PA 154 just north of Laporte. Follow PA 154 into Wyoming State Forest. After about 4 miles, turn left onto Shanerburg Road. Shanerburg Road is the first right along PA 154 heading from Worlds End State Park. Follow this road for about 1.5 miles until you reach a small parking area, where a gated forest road joins Shanerburg Road to your left. If you follow Shanerburg Road where it begins to bear right as it ascends the plateau, you have gone too far.

This beautiful loop is rarely visited by hikers, probably because it is part of the state forest's bridle trail system. Nevertheless, this trail offers plenty in the way of scenery and solitude. Also be prepared for numerous stream crossings.

From your car, follow the old forest road around the gate and across Shanerburg Run. This run is a beautiful mountain stream known for its brook trout; it flows through an undisturbed, natural setting. You soon reach the bridle trail's orange blazes. Follow the blazes to the right. Pole Bridge Trail is to the left (Hike No. 21). The trail stays close to the run and explores a scenic forest of hemlock, pine, and various hardwoods. Follow the trail across the run. When I first hiked this trail, I spotted a large white crane downstream. It was odd seeing a resplendent crane in a deep, dark forest.

The trail crosses the run again and reaches the first of many glades, a feature of this hike. You cross the stream two more times before reaching a large, scenic meadow with old apple trees. It is unusual to see an open area dominated by grass rather than ferns. It is possible that this meadow was once an orchard or farm. After passing through the meadow, the trail ascends and reaches another glade. Here, you see a small cascade. The trail crosses Rusty Run. A distinct, unblazed trail to your right follows Rusty Run upstream; this is a possible shortcut to Rusty Falls.

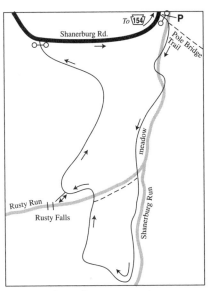

Hike 22: Shanerburg Run and Rusty Falls

The bridle trail follows Shanerburg Run for a short distance, passing a small flume, before it leaves the run permanently and makes a gradual ascent. You continue ascending through glades of ferns before descending beneath hemlocks. Follow the trail as it makes another sharp ascent to the right. The trail levels off in another glade. The two trails approaching from the left may go to Eagles Mere. Continue right again as the trail picks up a grassy, old forest road. Here, the trail descends, veers to the right, and apparently meets the shortcut trail described previously. Cross Rusty Run, turn left, and ascend again; the trail continues to follow the wide, old forest road. Pay attention where the trail turns right, because the blazes are infrequent. An unblazed trail to the left reaches scenic Rusty Falls after about 100 feet. The upper falls is about 6 feet high and plunges in a pool 3 feet deep. The lower falls is about 12 feet high. The name "rusty" is probably derived from the tannic acid coming from the swamps upstream and the hemlocks. This spot is ideal for a rest. Farther upstream, Rusty Run flows through the Rainbow Estate, formerly owned by L. E. Phipps, a wealthy exporter from New Jersey who used the place as his summer residence. The estate covered about 400 acres and had a dammed pond, a large "cottage," and a herd of deer corralled by the fence that surrounded the estate. The estate was named after Rainbow Falls, a 35-foot waterfall located on the property.

After returning to the bridle trail, follow the old forest road as it gently sweeps through the woods. The trail bears left and soon meets Shanerburg Road, on which you turn right for the descent to your car. Along the way, there are some broken views of the glen carved by Shanerburg Run and its tributaries.

23. Double Run Trail and Mineral Spring Falls

Duration: 2 to 3 hours

Distance: 4 miles

Difficulty: Moderate—most inclines and declines are moderate; stream crossings; rocky and slippery in sections

Highlights: Woodland hiking, mountain streams, waterfalls, sulfur spring

Elevation change: 400 feet

Directions: The trailhead is located about 2 miles south of Worlds End State Park along Double Run Road (SR 3009). Look for the Double Run Trail sign, or continue a short distance farther where Coal Mine Road meets Double Run Road; this is where the Loyalsock Trail (LT) crosses the road. Parking is extremely limited at the Double Run trailhead, but more parking is available where the LT crosses Double Run Road. If parking here is impossible, you can drive directly to Mineral Spring and hike the trail in reverse. Take Mineral Spring Road from the camping area in Worlds End. Continue past Cold Run Road to your left (which goes to Canyon Vista) and park near the state forest boundary sign, which is a short distance farther. You can see Mineral Spring Falls from the road.

Double Run Trail is a gated forest road and is blazed red; do not confuse it with Double Run Nature Trail at Worlds End. From the trailhead along Double Run Road, hike around the gate and follow the trail as it makes a gradual descent to Double Run. Here, the trail is infrequently blazed, but the old forest road is established. Double Run comes into view, as does the LT, which descends steeply from the bank to your right. The LT crosses Double Run Road a couple hundred feet above where you began the hike. You can also use the LT as a trailhead if parking is a problem.

The LT continues to follow the old forest road upstream and marks your return route. Now, however, follow Double Run Trail as it makes

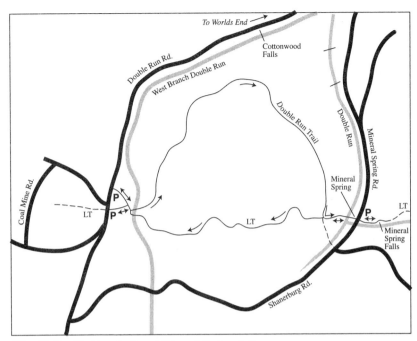

Hike 23: Double Run Trail and Mineral Spring Falls

a sharp left and crosses Double Run. Here, the trail is wide and grassy as it makes a moderate incline from the stream and turns left up the mountain. Like most state forests, Wyoming State Forest is laced with countless old forest roads and railroad grades that were used to mine and log what is now state forest land. The trail makes a gradual ascent as it climbs the ridge of the gorge above Double Run. The trail is wide and grassy for most of this portion of the hike. It can also be very wet where it crosses springs. In winter, there are broken views of the gorge and the plateau. Soon the red blazes are joined by orange blazes, indicating a bridle trail. The trail wanders through a hardwood forest interspersed with hemlocks. To your right, the trees are sparse—victims of windstorms, insect infestation, or logging. The trail makes a gradual descent and intersects with the LT, which you will use as a return route. The Double Run section of this hike is the least scenic portion, but it makes for a nice loop.

Turn left onto the LT and enter the woods. It feels odd to be on a narrow footpath after the wide, grassy forest road. Here, the trail is mostly level as it reaches the top of some bluffs. The LT descends the bluffs and passes a rock shelter underneath an overhang and protected by a stone wall. The LT then makes a gradual but rocky descent to Double Run and Mineral Spring. Soon the LT reaches the run in a scenic glen protected by hemlocks. Here, two streams descend in numerous cascades and small waterfalls and join together. Across Double Run is Mineral Spring, a sulfur spring that has colored the surrounding rocks a bright orange. If you get close enough, the sulfur smell is strong. When I was there last, there was quite a bit of water coming out of the spring. The LT climbs up to Mineral Spring Road and enters a rocky glen to Mineral Spring Falls, which has also been called Cold Run Road Falls. This waterfall is only about 25 feet high but is unusual, in that the water tumbles over a top ledge of about 2 feet, slides down a long flume or chute, and then makes its final drop into a small pool. The LT climbs to the left of the falls, which can be very slippery. Above, there are more cascades and another waterfall about 4 feet high. After enjoying the scenery, cross Mineral Spring Road and return to Double Run the way you came.

Before leaving Double Run, look downstream for a large boulder perched precariously on the bank. If you go to this boulder, you will see a large flume that slides over a rock face before entering a large pool. This flume would make a natural water slide, but some of the rock edges are jagged. From here, return to Double Run Trail the way you came.

Once you reach Double Run Trail, follow the LT for a more scenic return hike. At first, the LT is level, but then it makes a short but steep ascent up to Winner's Knob. At the top, there are broken views to the east of Double Run Gorge and the surrounding plateau. The LT then descends, crosses another forest road (which appears to be in use), and continues with a slight descent through a hardwood forest. Gradually, hemlocks begin to dominate as the trail nears and crosses a small tributary to the West Branch of Double Run, which the trail follows back to the West Branch via a railroad grade. The hemlocks here give the forest a deep, dark, and mysterious feel. The LT crosses the West Branch of Double Run, passes some campsites, and heads downstream on the grade. You soon return to where you started.

🚶🚶 24. Scar Run

Duration: 3 to 4 hours

Distance: 3 miles

Difficulty: Difficult—slippery and wet; off-trail hiking and bushwhacking along Scar Run; terrain can be rocky, steep, and eroded along the run, with blowdowns in sections

Highlights: Isolated, scenic gorge with waterfalls, cascades, flumes, and boulders

Elevation change: 700 feet

Directions: From Worlds End State Park, follow Double Run Road (SR 3009) south toward Eagles Mere for about 2.1 miles. Make the second right onto Coal Mine Road. Follow this road about 2.8 miles to Scar Run Trail on the left, a gated logging road; it is shortly after a power-line swath.

M uch likes its sister stream to the south, Ketchum Run (Hike No. 25), Scar Run is a place of great beauty. Scar Run has carved a scenic gorge into the plateau, creating many waterfalls and cascades. Because Scar Run is a relatively small stream, it is best to visit during periods of sufficient rain. Scar Run Trail is blazed red.

From Coal Mine Road, Scar Run Trail is actually a gated logging road. Fortunately, the surrounding forest has not been clear-cut. You may see a sign for the trail, but when I hiked here, the sign had been knocked over.

The logging road is mostly level as it crosses the top of the plateau. The surrounding forest is a mixture of hemlocks and hardwoods. Upon reaching an open area where four logging roads meet, continue straight. The logging road narrows and bears right, and faint red blazes begin to appear occasionally. The logging road ends, and the trail becomes an old forest grade with birch saplings. You begin a gradual descent among hemlocks after crossing a moss-covered, rotting wooden footbridge over a rivulet. Follow the blazes as the trail turns left toward Scar Run. From here, Scar Run Trail, which will be your return route, descends toward PA 87, high along the top of the gorge. To see Scar Run and its waterfalls, you have no choice but to bushwhack and hike along the stream.

After making the left turn, head off to your right toward one of Scar Run's branches. This is a small stream dotted with cobblestones. As you proceed downstream, the gradient increases, and there are cas-

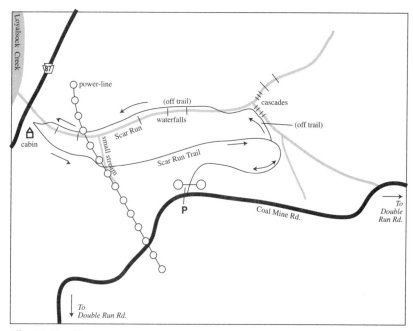

Hike 24: Scar Run

cades among the boulders and cobblestones. Be careful as you traverse this rocky, slippery terrain. The two branches of Scar Run unite in a scenic location. The branch you just hiked down is a staircase of cascades over moss-covered boulders; the other branch has a 20-foot waterfall with its own series of cascades. Another hidden 10-foot waterfall is just above the 20-foot falls.

You now proceed downstream along Scar Run. Fortunately, there is an old grade that follows the stream closely, making this streamside hike easier than others in this guide. At first the old grade is on the left (south) bank, but it crosses the stream when the left bank becomes too steep. The grade remains on the right bank for most of the hike. The gorge becomes increasingly deeper as Scar Run cascades over boulders and cobblestones beneath hemlocks. The run makes a sharp right turn where it plummets down a tight chasm into a small pool, creating a 15-foot waterfall. Follow the grade as it also descends along the stream. After a few hundred feet, the gorge narrows as boulders clog the streambed, and a rock face rises on the opposite bank. You pass a small, deep pool fed by a small, powerful cascade. Blowdowns are a problem along the grade, and in some places, the grade has been eroded away, so caution is required. The impressive scenery continues to another 20-foot waterfall and an awesome flume that shoots straight from the bottom of the falls for about 100 feet. It then tumbles into a shallow pool.

The grade continues downstream, passing more cascades, and crosses a power-line swath. Upon reentering the forest, you are treated to more boulder-formed cascades and a 6-foot waterfall. The forest here is a mix of hemlocks and hardwoods. You then reach another 20-foot waterfall, which also has a long, impressive flume that curves to the left. Here, the grade is above the run, but the beauty can be clearly seen.

Continue to follow the grade downstream, where it crosses the run and passes a hidden 7-foot waterfall to your right. The grade becomes a trail and meets the red-blazed Scar Run Trail behind a green hunting cabin. PA 87 is just ahead.

Turn left on Scar Run Trail as it ascends the side of the gorge beneath scenic hemlocks. The trail is an old forest road that is still in good condition. After .25 mile, the trail levels off as Scar Run flows far below to your left. You join the power-line swath you crossed previously, which offers a narrow view. The trail climbs up along the brier-choked swath. You meet another grade, and the trail turns left where it reenters the forest and crosses a rivulet. More blowdowns greet you, but the trail is level as mature hardwoods rise around you. The trail bears right at a Y with another grade and continues a mild ascent to the point where you began to bushwhack. Return the way you came.

25. Ketchum Run Gorge

Duration:	3 to 4 hours
Distance:	7 miles
Difficulty:	Very difficult—extremely rocky, rugged, and slippery in the gorge; numerous stream crossings; some sections steep and eroded; bushwhacking required to two off-trail waterfalls
Highlights:	Several sizable waterfalls, numerous small waterfalls and cascades, several large flumes, deep pools; scenic vistas; beautiful isolated gorge
Elevation change:	600 feet
Directions:	This isolated hike is difficult to reach, and there are three different ways to access it. This description uses the trailhead of the Barkshed Trail along High Knob Road. From Worlds End State Park, take Double Run Road

(SR 3009) south to Eagles Mere. After about 3 miles, a parking area and High Knob Road are located to your right. Turn right onto High Knob Road. Barkshed Trail is an old forest road whose trailhead is on the right, about 1.25 miles from Double Run Road. It is very easy to pass the trailhead, so watch for it. Unfortunately, parking is very limited here. If there is no place to park, you can go to the parking area at the juncture of Double Run Road and High Knob Road and reach Barkshed Trail via the Fern Rock Nature Trail (Hike No. 26). This may be your best choice. The most direct way into the gorge is to take Coal Mine Road, a single-lane dirt road. The second juncture of Coal Mine Road along Double Run Road is 2.1 miles south of Worlds End. Follow Coal Mine Road for 2 miles from Double Run Road to where it crosses the Loyalsock Trail (LT). You have to keep an eye out for the LT's blazes. There is sufficient parking along the road a few hundred feet before the LT crosses Coal Mine Road. Because the gorge is difficult to access, a loop trail is impossible, and you will have to retrace your steps. It is strongly suggested that you obtain a map of Wyoming State Forest for this hike or obtain trail maps of the LT from the Alpine Club of Williamsport.

Except for those who are familiar with the LT, Ketchum Run Gorge is an undiscovered gem of incredible natural beauty. It is also isolated; there is no road, or trail, that directly accesses the gorge from High Knob or Double Run Road. Despite its isolation, Ketchum Run has several scenic campsites and seems to be popular with hikers familiar with the area. Take the red-blazed Barkshed Trail as it follows an old forest road through some glades. The trail enters a hemlock forest; to your left is scenic Ketchum Run. Here, the trail is fairly level, but watch for rocks and root entanglements. The trail passes the blazes of Fern Rock Nature Trail, which crosses Barkshed Trail twice as it makes its loop through the forest.

The trail enters a mixed hardwood and hemlock forest and turns left when it intercepts a bridle trail. Both trails cross Ketchum Run as it slides over a rock face. A few feet downstream is a pretty waterfall about 5 feet high. Here, you have to make a decision. If you are a beginner, you may want to take Barkshed Trail as it follows an old forest road to the LT, which is still more than .5 mile away. The problem with this route is that this section of the Barkshed is poorly blazed, the trail is not very scenic, and there are many blowdowns. Plus, you have to make a right onto the LT and hike another .5 mile just to reach Ketchum Run again. If you are more experienced and wish to do some off-trail exploring, simply follow Ketchum Run downstream. There are no trails or blazes, so always stay close to the run. You may have to cross the run if one bank becomes too steep. Surprisingly, there are two sizable waterfalls along this uncharted section of Ketchum Run. After about .2 mile, there is a 15-foot waterfall where the run tumbles over a ledge and an accompanying boulder in two separate leaps. Just farther downstream is what appears to be the highest waterfall along Ketchum Run—a beautiful, narrow waterfall about 25 feet high that descends into a pool. Continue to follow the run downstream, passing more small waterfalls and flumes. You may have to hike around some blowdowns that cross the creek. After about .25 mile farther, you reach the LT as it crosses Ketchum Run in a hemlock grove. Keep an eye out for the LT's blazes. There are a few campsites here as well. You would have approached this spot on the LT if you had taken Barkshed Trail.

Follow the LT downstream through a forest predominated by hemlocks. Here the trail is fairly level. It crosses the North Branch of Ketchum Run and another small tributary after a short distance. Here the trail enters a large, grassy glade. There are campsites and a trail register. This is a nice place to take a break and read some of the notes in the register, almost all of which comment on the beauty of this gorge. To the left are remains of an old splash dam. In the logging era, splash dams were used to gather water, which was then released to float logs downstream. Splash dams were commonly used along streams that were too small to float logs.

The trail passes through the glade and hugs the bank of Ketchum Run. Here the trail is heavily eroded, and you have to scramble along the edge of the bank. Ketchum Run enters a rocky mini-gorge with several long, impressive flumes. Although rugged, this section of the trail is particularly scenic, with cliffs and ledges. The trail reaches the top of 15-foot Lee's Falls. The LT turns sharply to the right as it ascends a steep bank; follow the red X (RX) trail down to the base of the falls and across the run to the other side. This part of the hike is steep, rocky, and very difficult. It requires several stream crossings that can be tricky in high water, so use caution. The RX trail passes in front of a huge landslide on the other bank that reaches almost the top of the gorge. Around you, Ketchum Run swirls and roars in continuous rapids and small waterfalls. The RX trail continues to follow the run downstream and crosses it again through incredible scenery. The trail begins to ascend the bank and meets the LT. Turn left on the LT as it descends the bank and follows the run downstream. To the left you should hear the roar of a small, powerful waterfall that rushes between two large boulders into a deep pool—a typical sight along this hike.

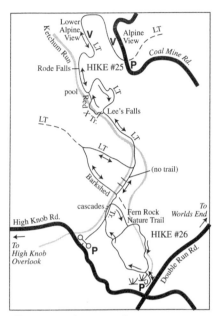

Hike 25: Ketchum Run Gorge
Hike 26: Fern Rock Nature Trail

The LT continues downstream and passes a small waterfall before it reaches the top of 20-foot Rode Falls (named after Ruth Rode, a longtime member of the Alpine Club of Williamsport), which tumbles over a ledge into a deep pool. Climb down the ladder alongside the falls and take a rest at the campsite at the foot of the falls. From here, the LT begins to ascend the side of the gorge and leaves Ketchum Run. The trail turns right and ascends via old railroad grades and forest roads. The trail levels and arrives at Lower Alpine View, which offers a nice view of the twisting Loyalsock Creek and its valley. This vista is perched on top of a cliff that is gradually separating from the mountainside, as demonstrated by a fracture line behind the vista. The LT is level, bears left on an old forest road, and then turns right to begin the climb to the top of the plateau. You pass through some areas with briers and bushes to reach Alpine View, another beautiful view of the Loyalsock and Ketchum Run Gorge. This vista also has a grassy area that would make a decent campsite. If you parked on Coal Mine Road, the road is .3 mile farther; otherwise, you will have to turn around and retrace your steps.

On your return, follow the LT and avoid the RX trail, unless you want to rehike the same trail back. If you remember, the LT avoided Ketchum Run above Lee's Falls and met up with the RX trail (which you hiked) about .6 mile farther. Once you reach this point on your hike back, follow the LT as it turns left from the RX trail and follows an old grade up the bank. The LT makes a sharp right and continues to ascend the bank. The trail passes through some hemlocks and comes to Jack's Window, which offers a narrow view of Lee's Falls below. The trail takes a switchback up the bank, levels off, and passes above the landslide noted previously. The trail turns right and makes a sharp descent back to Ketchum Run and the top of Lee's Falls.

From here, simply retrace your steps back to the Fern Rock Nature Trail trailhead or the Barkshed trailhead along High Knob Road, depending on where you parked.

26. Fern Rock Nature Trail

Duration:	1¹/₂ to 2 hours

Distance: 2 miles

Difficulty: Easy—very rocky in parts and may be slippery near Ketchum Run

Highlights: Pleasant woodland hike, small cascades and pools along Ketchum Run, self-guided nature trail with numbered stations

Elevation change: 100 ft.

Directions: The trailhead is located at the parking area where Double Run Road and High Knob Road meet. The parking area is about 3 miles south of Worlds End State Park and 4 miles north of Eagles Mere.

This is an ideal hike for beginners or young children. The terrain is mostly flat but rocky, and the trail is blazed with orange circles with the blue letters "FR." The trail was begun by Scouts from nearby Camp Lycogis, continued by students at Sullivan County High School, and completed in the late 1970s by crews of the local Youth Conservation Corps. Today the trail is maintained by Wyoming State Forest. The trail is a 2-mile loop with a shortcut trail about halfway. The trail has 31 stations that offer insights into the surrounding forest. Make sure to pick up a brochure at the trailhead.

The trail passes by several different habitats, including swamps, streams, clearings, and forest. The trail descends from the parking area and passes to the right of a large swamp. After passing stations 1 through 6, cross the creek and turn left to begin the loop. The trail goes around the other side of the swamp through a beautiful verdant forest of hemlock and ground pine. Eventually the trail passes through hardwoods. The forest is a mix of hard- and softwoods and includes hemlock, red maple, yellow birch, moosewood or striped maple, black cherry, American beech, and sugar maple. There is also plenty of wildlife. You may see chipmunks and squirrels racing across the trail or deer leaping through the forest. Between stations 13 and 14, there is an orange-blazed shortcut trail with a blue "S." This trail takes you to the other side of the loop and shortens your hike by about 45 minutes.

At the far end of the loop, the trail crosses Barkshed Trail (see Hike No. 25) and descends to Ketchum Run. Here the run has several small waterfalls, chutes, and flumes and a few deep pools harboring brook trout. This is one of the most scenic sections of the hike. The trail leaves Ketchum Run, crosses Barkshed Trail again, and makes its way back to the trailhead. The trail passes by a large boulder and is soon joined by the shortcut trail, which is easy to miss. Make sure you pay attention to the blazes on your return, because it is easy to miss the trail in spots. The trail continues to be rocky as it passes under hemlocks and crosses several streams. You complete the loop at the first bridge. Turn left and cross the bridge to reach the parking area.

 27. High Knob Overlook

Duration:	4 to 5 hours
Distance:	6.75 miles

Difficulty: Moderate to difficult—long ascent for about 1 mile at the beginning of the hike; steep ascent to High Knob; often wet, rocky, and eroded in spots

Highlights: Famous vista, mountain bogs, diverse forests, waterfalls

Elevation change: 1,100 feet

Directions: Proceed north on PA 87 from the Montoursville exit of US 220/I-180 for about 21.6 miles; Dry Run Road is on your right. There is a sign for the Dry Run Picnic Area. Turn right onto Dry Run Road, follow it for several hundred yards, and park at the ranger station. If you're heading south on PA 87, Dry Run Road is on the left, about 1.5 miles south of Hillsgrove.

High Knob Trail is blazed orange as well as red, indicating that it is also a bridle trail. The trail leaves Dry Run Road and the ranger station up a wide, grassy forest road. It makes a long, steady ascent for about a mile. Here, hardwoods dominate the forest, with an interspersed understory of mountain laurel. The trail passes a small seasonal stream as it tumbles down a ravine and enters a wide, grassy area. The trail turns left and makes another ascent to a beautiful forest of white pine with a thick understory of young pine trees. Some of the white pine trees are sizable.

Originally, it was Jackson Trail, not High Knob Trail, that went to High Knob. This confusing setup was changed so that High Knob Trail would reach its namesake. Before continuing on High Knob Trail, make a left on Jackson Trail (and the grassy forest road) and follow it for about 100 yards. You will reach Duck Pond, a small mountaintop bog. If you enjoy watching wildlife, this is the place to do it.

Back on High Knob Trail, you pass through hemlocks, pines, and thick stands of laurel. The trail also crosses several springs. You arrive at another, larger bog off to your left. Here, the forest is especially diverse and scenic. The trail veers to the right and reenters the hardwood forest. After about .5 mile, the trail goes through another thicket of mountain laurel and some hemlock and white pine; you will see a sign for Nettle Ridge Trail, which begins along PA 87, passes down in front of High Knob Overlook, and intersects the Loyalsock Trail (LT) .5 mile south of the overlook. The trail then makes a slight descent and scrambles over a small ledge. When I first hiked this trail, the portion from the ledge to the overlook was virtually impenetrable—hundreds of sizable trees had blown down, and the brier bushes were almost carnivorous. The trail makes another ascent, crosses a bridle trail, and makes a steep, eroded ascent to High Knob Overlook.

High Knob Overlook is one of the most popular destinations in the state forest. The view it offers when the mountain laurel is blooming and during the fall foliage season is breathtaking. Seven counties can

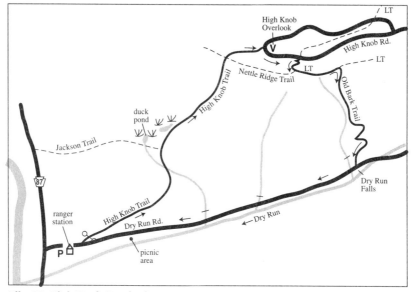

Hike 27: High Knob Overlook

be seen from the overlook. The high plateau that spreads out in front of the vista is deeply indented with gorges and canyons. Camp, Gooseberry, and Bear Mountains surround the overlook, and Loyalsock Creek flows 1,000 feet below. Like most people, I first visited High Knob via car; High Knob Road provides direct access to the overlook. As a result, few people hike scenic High Knob Trail. Reaching the overlook by trail is definitely more rewarding. To the east, over Gooseberry Mountain, it is possible to see another famous vista, Sharp Top (Hike No. 42).

From here, you have two choices: You can return the way you came, or you can hike a loop using part of Dry Run Road. Although walking along a road is not ideal, Dry Run Road offers a nice cooldown and passes by waterfalls and cascades.

To hike the loop from the overlook, turn left (as if looking from the overlook) and proceed south along High Knob Road. As you walk along the edge of the road, you are treated to more views. After about .25 mile, you should see blazes for the LT on the right side of the road. Jump over the guardrail, and there is yet another view. The LT makes a sharp descent via well-constructed switchbacks. Once you reach the bottom, the red-blazed Nettle Ridge Trail joins the LT. Follow the LT for about .3 mile, and you come to Old Bark Trail on the right; use this trail for the descent to Dry Run Road. At first, the trail crosses a few blowdowns and springs, and the blazes are intermittent. However, the blazes soon become more frequent. Off to the right is a small seasonal stream. The trail crosses an old forest road and follows another grassy forest road down to Dry Run Road. The descent is fairly gradual, but there are a few blowdowns. You are also offered some views of the small stream as it softly cascades down its ravine. The trail leaves the ravine as it twists down to Dry Run. Right before you reach Dry Run Road, look up the small stream to see a hidden waterfall about 20 feet high. This waterfall is best viewed during wet weather. Across Dry Run Road is yet another waterfall, Dry Run Falls. This scenic waterfall tumbles into a pool and has a few picnic tables nearby, making it an ideal resting spot.

The remainder of the hike is down Dry Run Road. This road is open to cars, and traffic may be heavy during weekends in the summer and fall. However, the motorists rarely see the beauty around them. To the left is Dry Run as it tumbles and swirls down to Loyalsock Creek. To the right are small feeder streams with their many cascades. You soon arrive at the Dry Run Picnic Area on your left. The ranger station and your car are only .5 mile farther.

28. Dutter's Run and Ryan's Trail

Duration: 3¹/₂ hours

Distance: 6 miles

Difficulty: Difficult—the Loyalsock Trail (LT) segment is moderate, briers are a nuisance along a few sections, and there are moderate inclines and declines; the Ryan's Trail segment is difficult, some sections are steep and eroded, there is a longer ascent, and some blazes are faded and infrequent. High Landing Trail is often wet and has briers.

Highlights: Mary's View, waterfalls and cascades along Dutter's Run, Kettle Creek Gorge, swamps and bogs

Elevation change: 600 feet

Directions: Proceeding north along PA 87 from the Montoursville exit for about 21.6 miles, Dry Run Road is on your right. There is a sign for the Dry Run Picnic Area. Turn right onto Dry Run Road. Proceeding south along PA 87, Dry Run Road is on the left, about 1.5 miles south of Hillsgrove. Follow Dry Run Road for about 3 miles. Watch for where the LT crosses the road; there is a small parking area on your left.

This hike traverses a scenic portion of the popular LT, as well as Ryan's and High Landing Trails, two isolated trails that are rarely hiked. Follow the LT across Dry Run Road and into a hardwood forest. If it has been raining, expect a wet hike, as there are numerous stream crossings and the trail follows several springs. Here, the trail is mostly flat and tunnels through patches of omnipresent briers. Off to the left, the forest has been logged or salvaged, with several scags left standing—a somewhat familiar sight along the LT. This is probably the result of an insect infestation that killed off many trees.

You arrive at scenic Mary's View and its register, overlooking the distinctive V of Dry Run Gorge. To the west rises the point of Smith's Knob, and to the northwest (right) is High Knob. Bushes of mountain laurel surround this site, making it an ideal place to visit in June when the laurel blooms.

The trail continues and passes some large boulders off to the left. You begin a descent toward Dutter's Run, a small stream with numerous cascades. Be forewarned: The LT crosses this stream at least four times. The stream tumbles over several 4- to 5-foot waterfalls and several flumes within a small gorge. The trail rounds a bend in the stream and comes upon 10-foot Dutter's Run Falls, which plummets over a

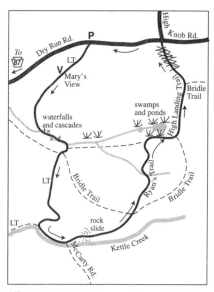

Hike 28: Dutter's Run and Ryan's Trail

broad ledge. The LT continues upstream, passing in front of another 4-foot waterfall and a campsite, and ascends the side of the gorge. The trail makes a sharp right and follows close to the edge of the gorge. After a short distance, the LT crosses Dutter's Run Trail, an old forest road.

The trail stays level as it passes through a beautiful hardwood forest. After crossing some springs, the trail intersects with McCarty Road, another old forest road, and makes a short ascent to another stretch of dead trees and carnivorous briers (this section was especially difficult to pass through). The trail bears left and leaves the briers. You finally arrive at Kettle Creek Gorge, to which the LT descends via some steep switchbacks.

Upon reaching the bottom of the gorge, the trail meets unblazed McCarty Road again. The LT turns right and follows McCarty Road downstream. Do not follow the LT; instead, make a left onto McCarty Road and follow it for a short distance (see Hike No. 30). The road fords Kettle Creek and passes some campsites. Do not cross Kettle Creek. To your left you will see a sign for Ryan's Trail, which is blazed red. Follow Ryan's Trail as it stays close to Kettle Creek. On the other bank, the creek flows up against a thick wall of sandstone. Soon you will notice a massive cliff to your left; this is the most treacherous section of Ryan's Trail. The trail crosses a steep bank of loose rock and goes through several blowdowns directly above Kettle Creek. Use extreme caution while negotiating this section. If you find it impassable, you have no choice but to cross to the other bank of Kettle Creek. Even this route is difficult, as Kettle Creek has eroded the sandstone, creating steep banks of solid stone.

From this point, Ryan's Trail is considerably easier, with the biggest obstacles being blowdowns and infrequent or faded blazes. The trail follows an old railroad grade up the gorge and passes through an open area dominated by briers. Ryan's Trail reenters the forest as it explores the upper portion of beautiful Kettle Creek Gorge. The gorge is isolated, has a graceful shape, and is dominated by hardwoods. Off to your right, scenic Kettle Creek reminds you of its presence. I've been told that there is a waterfall along Kettle Creek in this vicinity. The trail leaves the creek and makes a steep ascent up the gorge. Here, the trail is blazed fairly well, but there is little indication of an established trail. Ryan's Trail levels off as it traverses the edge of a bench within the gorge. Soon the trail makes a slight descent. Be careful here, as there are no double blazes where the trail makes a sharp left. After making another ascent, the trail bears right and follows the edge of another bench within the gorge. You may have some trouble following the blazes here, especially when there are leaves on the trees. The trail makes a sharp left and another steep ascent and then levels off where the trail bears right. Ryan's Trail soon intercepts and follows an old forest or jeep road, which is level at first but then makes a gradual ascent past several springs. After leveling off once again, the trail leaves the jeep road. Here, the blazes are especially hidden. If you can't find them, try heading straight from the blaze on the back side of the tree. The trail makes another steep ascent, and the blazes continue to be obscure, but they're there.

The trail finally reaches the top of the gorge and meets a forest road, on which you turn left. Ryan's Trail enters an open area where trees are being replanted; it's almost odd to be in an area dominated by grass rather than briers. The trail crosses a bridle trail, and you'll see a sign for Ryan's Trail as it continues along a deer fence. I once hiked this section in winter without snowshoes when the snowdrifts were almost 2 feet deep—not one of the smartest things I've ever done.

The trail leaves the fence and enters the forest. It curves left and then slowly bears right when it crosses one of the branches of Dutter's Run. The run soon returns as it flows to your left, and Ryan's Trail ends at its intersection with High Landing Trail. This trail is an old forest road. If you want to shorten your hike, turn left on High Landing Trail, which intersects both McCarty Road and the LT near Dutter's Run.

Otherwise, turn right onto High Landing Trail. To your left is a large wetland from which another branch of Dutter's Run flows. High Landing Trail is level and often wet as it passes through the forest. After about .5 mile, the trail passes another swamp. This scenic wetland contains stunted pine trees and is an ideal place to view wildlife. The trail curves around the swamp and crosses its headwaters; this section is particularly wet. After crossing the headwaters, the trail follows an old forest road, makes a gradual ascent through a hardwood forest, and bears right. Here, the bridle trail proceeds straight, and the trail makes a left. This last portion of the trail is very frustrating. First, the trail proceeds through a horrendous stretch of briers. Second, the few trees that are left standing have faded blazes, which are spaced very far apart. The best advice I can give is to follow the blazes as best you can and proceed straight to Dry Run Road. Near some isolated hemlocks, the trail picks up an old ATV trail, descends to Dry Run, and ascends the bank to Dry Run Road. If this section is impenetrable, you can reach Dry Run Road via a grove of hemlocks a few hundred feet to your right. Once you reach the road, turn left and walk about .75 mile to your car.

29. Stony Run Trail

Duration: 2 to 3 hours

Distance: 3 miles

Difficulty: Moderate—rocky and wet, with long, gradual inclines and declines; some off-trail navigation and bushwhacking required

Highlights: Small stream with numerous cascades, mountain laurel, isolation

Elevation change: 800 feet

Directions: Proceeding north along PA 87 from the Montoursville exit for about 21.6 miles, Dry Run Road is on your right. There is a sign for the Dry Run Picnic Area. Turn right onto Dry Run Road, follow it for several hundred yards, and park at the ranger station. Proceeding south along PA 87, Dry Run Road is on the left, about 1.5 miles south of Hillsgrove.

This scenic loop begins at the Hillsgrove ranger station, which is also the starting point for the High Knob hike (Hike No. 27). Follow the orange blazes for the bridle trail that pass to the right of the station and a small radio tower. The trail fords Dry Run, and red blazes join the trail. Crossing Dry Run in high water can be very difficult. The trail passes behind some cabins and curves uphill into a beautiful grove of sizable hemlocks and white pines. You arrive at Stony Run Trail to your right; Old House Trail continues straight and will be your return route. Turn right onto Stony Run Trail, which is blazed red. The trail leaves the grove of pines and hemlocks and joins an old grade at the bottom of a large talus slope. Talus slopes are more commonly found in the ridge and valley region of central Pennsylvania. The trail is level but very rocky.

Hike 29: Stony Run Trail

The trail leaves the talus slope and passes through a hardwood forest with a thick understory of mountain laurel. Stony Run can be heard off to your right as it flows beneath hemlocks and pines. After burrowing through more laurel, the trail makes a sharp descent and crosses Stony Run. This run is small and probably disappears in the summer, so I suggest you hike this trail in midspring or late fall, when there is water and the cascades are best seen. The trail ascends the other bank and joins an old forest road high above Stony Run. The trail is wide and begins a long, gradual ascent under the shelter of occasional hemlocks. Beneath you, Stony Run cascades over ledges and in between large rocks. These cascades become more pronounced higher in the glen. The trail soon leaves the edge of the glen, and as a result, Stony Run disappears from view. This is unfortunate, because the run climaxes with a staircase of cascades beneath hemlocks and laurels near the top of the glen. It may be best if you just hike along the edge of the glen and then return to the trail.

The trail levels off, passes through more laurel, and enters a hardwood forest. Here, the trail is surprisingly well established as it traverses the laurel, probably due to deer rather than hikers. You turn left and cross the headwaters of Stony Run. The trail then ascends to near the top of the plateau, with large exposed boulders of sandstone and conglomerate.

When you reach the place where the blazes make a sharp right, stop. According to the state forest map, Stony Run Trail should meet Old House Trail here, or at least nearby, but it does not. In reality, Stony Run Trail makes the sharp right and heads off to Dutter's Trail, passing an old sign for Snake Trail; Old House Trail doesn't intersect for some distance. However, there is no reason to fear; simply cut straight through the forest (there is no trail or blazes) heading north. Pass some rocks and boulders and make a short descent to a bench, or flat area, above Dry Run Gorge. You will intercept Old House Trail after several hundred feet, which traverses the edge of Dry Run Gorge. Turn left onto Old House Trail, which is blazed red and yellow. To your right, the mountainside descends steeply to Dry Run.

After a short distance, you pass a sign for Dry Run Trail where it descends to the Dry Run Picnic Area. Old House Trail begins a long, rocky descent and arrives at its intersection with Stony Run Trail. Return the way you came.

30. Angel Falls and Kettle Creek Gorge

Duration:	4 hours
Distance:	7.5 miles
Difficulty:	Difficult—steep, slippery, rocky; off-trail hiking; several stream crossings; bushwhacking
Highlights:	Several beautiful waterfalls, overlook, streamside hiking
Elevation change:	750 feet

Directions: Proceeding north on US 220 from Hughesville, turn left onto PA 42 at Muncy Valley. Follow PA 42 for about 3 miles and turn left onto Brunnerdale Road, a dirt road. Follow Brunnerdale Road for about 4 miles; along the way, you pass Hunters Lake to your right. Before you get to Ogdonia Road, the parking area is on the right. From PA 87, Ogdonia Road is a little over a mile south of Dry Run Road, where the picnic area and ranger station are located. Turn onto Ogdonia Road and follow it for about 3.5 miles; then head left onto Brunnerdale Road. The parking area is about .25 farther, on the left.

This hike is one of the most scenic Wyoming State Forest has to offer. This trail utilizes portions of the Loyalsock Trail (LT) and is located in a beautiful, isolated spot with numerous gorges and glens. Follow the LT down along the right side of Ogdonia Run through a hemlock forest to where it meets Brunnerdale Run. Cross Brunnerdale Run as best you can, still following the LT, which makes a left and follows Ogdonia Run. The trail stays fairly close to Ogdonia Run for about .25 mile. The trail eventually moves away from the run, crosses a small spring, and rises over a small bank, where it meets an old forest road. Here, the LT makes a sharp right up the forest road; do not follow it. Instead, turn left onto the unblazed forest road and follow it through a mixed hemlock and hardwood forest. There is a discernible trail on this old road. The trail crosses several springs, and there are a few blowdowns.

The LT used to go this way, until it was rerouted to avoid the fragile habitats in Angels Falls glen. Camping, rock climbing, and rappelling are prohibited around Angel Falls; however, hiking is still permitted. It is unfortunate that the LT was rerouted, because this is by far the most scenic approach to Angel Falls. Currently, the LT is connected to Angel Falls by a blue-blazed spur trail. The problem with this setup is that the three waterfalls below Angel Falls are completely avoided. When you do reach Angel Falls,

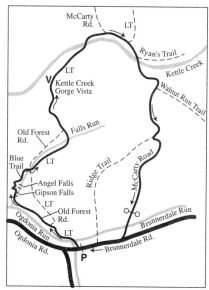

Hike 30: Angel Falls and Kettle Creek Gorge

please do not camp or disturb any vegetation, as the falls area has suffered from erosion.

The trail soon rejoins Ogdonia Run and passes an old campsite. Camping here is now prohibited to protect the downstream water supply. The trail then rises over a small bank and enters the glen carved by Falls Run, a small stream that can be reduced to a trickle in the summer. Don't be disappointed if there is no water in Falls Run down here, because there is usually at least some flowing over the waterfalls. Follow Falls Run upstream, staying to the right of it. You will see a sign stating the policy mentioned earlier. There is a faint trail up the glen, and you can see some old LT blazes that have been painted over. You have to cross Falls Run to the left. Up ahead, there is a 15-foot waterfall that descends over a broad ledge. There is no trail at this point, so to reach this waterfall, you have to scramble up the bank or streambed. Always stay on the left (west) side of the glen, and be careful as you negotiate the steep, leaf-filled banks. Climb the bank over the first waterfall, and as you ascend the edge of the glen, you can see several large, flat, flaking boulders. Pass to the right of these boulders and back down into the glen. The terrain is rugged, rocky, and steep; you may see a faint trail. You then come to Gipson Falls, the second-highest falls, at about 30 feet. Gipson Falls squeezes between two hemlocks at its crest and tumbles over several ledges. To the right of the falls, several springs tumble from a rock face.

Retrace your steps and climb up the edge of the glen. Use caution, as there are steep drop-offs to your right. You soon reach the blue-blazed spur trail that leads to the bottom and top of Angel Falls. Turn right on this trail and follow it to the foot of Angel Falls. The terrain here is very rocky. Angel Falls is about 80 feet high and was supposedly named by someone who had seen Angel Falls in Venezuela—the highest waterfall in the world, at over 3,000 feet—and thought this waterfall looked like a miniature. Immediately below Angel Falls, you can see the top of another small but inaccesible waterfall. To your left, you can see a perfectly straight, white rock face cut in a 90-degree angle in one place. It appears that some quarrying may have occurred here in the past.

Follow the blue-blazed trail up the switchbacks to the top of Angel Falls. The trail passes through a small grove of hemlock, rhododendron, and mountain laurel as it approaches the crest of Angel Falls. From the top of the falls, you are rewarded with a beautiful view of the glen and Ogdonia Gorge. Be careful not to venture too close to the edge of the cliff face. A few years ago, a girl was seriously injured when she fell from the top of the falls. Also, revegetation efforts are under way here, so stay on the trail.

From the falls, follow the blue blazes upstream and climb the bank via some switchbacks. The trail leads to a grassy forest road. If you so desire, you can follow this old forest road, which intersects with the LT before it descends into Kettle Creek Gorge, but there are several blowdowns. Continue to follow the blue blazes up this road for a short distance. The trail makes a right and leaves the road. It descends to Falls Run, scampers up the bank on the other side, and meets the LT. If you want to take a short loop hike, you can turn right onto the LT, and it will take you back to where you started. To see Kettle Creek Gorge and Vista, turn left onto the LT, which is clearly blazed.

The LT follows the bank above Falls Run and eventually crosses it, passing a small campsite. The trail follows the run almost to its source. The LT then makes a left and crosses the same old forest road discussed previously. The trail ascends over the rim of Kettle Creek Gorge and passes through a tunnel of young birch trees. As it descends into the gorge, the trail is narrow and steep and burrows through briers and bushes. The trail eventually begins to level a bit and passes a few springs. This part of the trail is rocky and can be slippery. The trail finally becomes level. At a blue sign for Kettle Creek Vista, turn left and hike a short distance to the vista.

Most vistas offer a view from the top of a mountain or a gorge. This vista offers a view from within the gorge, as it is located about halfway down into it. As a result, you get the feeling that you are completely surrounded by the gorge. The forested gorge has a graceful shape, and you can hear Kettle Creek below. There is also a nice campsite here.

Back on the LT, the trail is level, but you may have to scramble around some blowdowns. The LT begins to make a moderate, rocky descent to Kettle Creek and passes through more briers, which disappear once the trail reenters the forest. The trail descends to the bottom of the gorge and crosses scenic Kettle Creek. I've been told that there is a waterfall downstream along Kettle Creek, off the trail. This creek is a wilderness trout stream; in fact, 12-inch specimens have been caught here. During periods of high water, fording Kettle Creek can be tricky, if not dangerous. The trail scrambles up the bank and proceeds upstream. You soon pass a nice campsite and a small waterfall as it tumbles over a broad ledge. The LT uses an old railroad grade up Kettle Creek, which is always nearby to your right. A narrow-gauge railroad used to follow this grade, providing transportation to Eagles Mere and Sonestown in the early 1900s.

The railroad grade then merges with an old forest road, McCarty Road, which approaches from the left. McCarty Road is not passable to cars and is actually a wide, grassy trail. This old forest road is your return hike back to Brunnerdale Road and your car. The LT soon leaves unblazed McCarty Road and scrambles up a steep bank to the left; continue to follow McCarty Road to Kettle Creek. You will see a sign for the red-blazed Ryan's Trail to your left (see Hike No. 28). The trail (McCarty Road) fords Kettle Creek again and passes a couple of campsites. The second half of this hike is not nearly as scenic as the first half.

The trail begins to ascend the side of the gorge and is grassy and covered with ferns. You soon pass a section where the trail has been heavily eroded; it looks as if a retaining wall collapsed. The trail then passes a sign for the red-blazed Walnut Trail. This woodland hike also leads to Brunnerdale Road, but you would have to walk down the road for 2 miles just to reach your car. The trail continues to gain altitude for over a mile, and there are several blowdowns. As it reaches the top of the mountain, there is a large treeless area dominated by ferns. Ridge Trail is to the right; this red-blazed trail also descends to Brunnerdale Road and comes out close to the parking area. However, it is infrequently blazed, and there are numerous blowdowns.

From here, McCarty Road makes a moderate descent of the mountain. At the bottom, it passes a cabin, crosses Brunnerdale Run, and ends at Brunnerdale Road. Turn right onto Brunnerdale Road and follow it about .5 mile to your car.

31. Hunters Lake (Pennsylvania Fish and Boat Commission)

Duration:	1 to 2 hours
Distance:	3 miles
Difficulty:	Easy—mostly level; portions are rocky, entangled with roots, and wet
Highlights:	Lakeside views, Hunters Lake
Elevation change:	100 feet

Directions: From US 220, turn onto Route 42 at Muncy Valley toward Eagles Mere. After almost 3 miles, you reach the top of the plateau and make the second left onto Brunnerdale Road; there is a sign for Hunters Lake. Follow this road for about .75 mile. Hunters Lake is on your right; the large parking area is on your left.

Contact information: Pennsylvania Fish and Boat Commission, Northeast Regional Office, PO Box 88, Sweet Valley, PA 18656; phone: 570-477-2206 or 570-477-5717; website: www.fish.state.pa.us

From the parking area, cross Brunnerdale Road and walk across the dam. Hunters Lake is a beautiful lake owned by the Pennsylvania Fish and Boat Commission. Its graceful shoreline is virtually undeveloped, and the lake is surrounded by wooded slopes. The scenery of this lake is comparable to, if not better than, that of Eagles Mere Lake, but more importantly, you are likely to have Hunters Lake all to yourself. Even if you're not a hiker, Hunters Lake is a great place to go fishing, bird-watching, or kayaking.

Few hikers know that there is a blazed trail on the east side of the lake. This trail, blazed gold, usually stays close to the lake and offers many views of it. Although the trail is blazed fairly well, there are sections where it is relatively unestablished.

After reaching the other end of the dam, turn left into the woods. You will immediately see the gold blazes. The diverse forest contains hemlock, maple, oak, and beech. The trail crosses a spring and turns left toward the lake. You then turn away from the lake and join an old

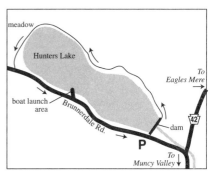

Hike 31: Hunters Lake

forest road, which enters a hemlock grove with large rocks. Through this area you may see some beaver activity around the lake; there are many chiseled trees along the hike. The trail turns left and meets the lake, only to turn right away from it again. Cross over another spring and small stream. When you reach the edge of the lake, there's a nice view over it. Across the lake you can see the boat launch.

Follow the trail as it moves away from the lake and passes a large, rounded boulder. You soon return to the lake, descending along a tricky, leaf-filled bank. Cross over more springs and small streams, enjoying the nice views of the lake. You soon reach my favorite spot, where a fallen log sits underneath hemlocks as you look out over the lake. The glistening water on a clear fall day is a memorable sight. The trail stays very close to the lake. From here, you can see the dam and North Mountain rising prominently to the southeast. The trail leaves the forest, turns left, and crosses a concrete walkway across an open meadow. There are great views down the lake and of North Mountain. This walkway is actually a small dam, or retaining wall, to prevent Hunters Lake from spilling over and flowing north into the Rock Run watershed. From here, follow the gated road to Brunnerdale Road, on which you turn left, and hike a little over a mile back to your car.

🥾 32. Laurel Ridge Trail

Duration: 2¹/₂ hours

Distance: 3 miles

Difficulty: Moderate—begins with a long incline; poorly blazed in parts; isolated, rocky, eroded, and sometimes wet, particularly on the return

Highlights: Vistas of the surrounding plateau, unique forest types, mountain laurel and wildlife

Elevation change: 600 feet

Directions: From US 220, turn onto Route 42 at Muncy Valley toward Eagles Mere. After almost 3 miles, you reach the top of the plateau and make the second left onto Brunnerdale Road; there is a sign for Hunters Lake. Follow Brunnerdale Road for about 3.5 miles. Along the way, you pass Hunters Lake to your right, cross Rock Run, and pass the Walnut Trail trailhead, also on your right. Soon thereafter you see a gated forest road on your left and a sign indicating that this is the beginning of Laurel Ridge Trail. The trailhead is easy to miss. There is space for only about two cars.

This is a semiloop hike. You can begin either here or about .4 mile farther, where the trail returns to Brunnerdale Road.

If you enjoy isolation, this is the hike for you. The trail is rarely hiked and is probably used mostly by sportsmen during hunting season. Hike around the gate and continue your ascent up the forest road. There are no blazes; simply follow the forest road. Almost immediately you will notice logging activity. The first half of this hike passes a section of forest that has been either logged or salvaged. Although most hikers cringe at the thought of logging, it provides some nice vistas and a chance to view wildlife, since many species are attracted to open areas.

Continue the long, moderate ascent up the mountain. An old forest road comes in from the right, and the red blazes finally begin. They aren't a whole lot of help, however, because they are intermittent. Simply follow the forest road, and you'll be on track. To the right up the hillside, all the dead trees were left standing to serve as den trees. Be prepared to be startled by grouse along this open stretch of trail. The trail continues uphill, makes a sharp right, and then makes a slight ascent to an open area filled with scags. Here you are provided with the first vista. In winter, the silvery scags and the deep snow give this section of the hike an almost surreal feel. The trail turns left for a few hundred feet and then makes a sharp right up the hill, following another grade. The lack of blazes may make this section difficult to navigate.

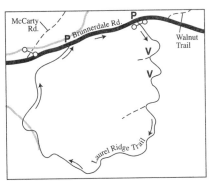

Hike 32: Laurel Ridge Trail

Follow the trail uphill, and you'll notice more faded blazes. Here you are treated to an even nicer view; to the northeast you can see Eagles Mere. The trail proceeds uphill and curves right and serves as a border between hemlocks and the logged area. The forest road continues straight; however, you should proceed left onto an old woods road and enter the hemlock forest. Here the blazes appear with more consistency. When I hiked this trail last, I came across countless deer along this section.

There is a sharp contrast between the open, logged area and the dense, green hemlock forest through which the trail now passes. It makes a gradual ascent and passes some laurel thickets. The trail then curves right as it climbs to the top of the ridge; blowdowns may be a problem here. Soon the trail reaches the top—a scenic area dominated by oak trees with a thick understory of mountain laurel that crowds the trail. This is the trail's namesake, and when the laurel is in bloom, this section is beautiful.

The trail makes a sharp left and begins its descent through a forest dominated by hemlocks and pines. This section is overblazed, in stark contrast to the beginning of the hike. The trail passes the edge of a glade bordered by hemlocks. Turn left, and the trail returns to an old forest road and descends along a seasonal streambed. The trail is somewhat eroded and passes a few blowdowns. Here the trail winds gradually down the mountain, passing by springs and a small stream. The trail turns right, crosses a small stream, and levels out. Along this section is where I saw tracks of the elusive bobcat, but unfortunately, I didn't see their creator. To the left are some boulders and rock faces. The trail turns right and offers a broken view of Ogdonia Run Gorge in winter. From here, the trail makes a gradual descent to Brunnerdale Road. Once you arrive at the road, turn right. Your car is .4 mile farther.

33. Middle Branch Trail

Duration: 3 hours

Distance: 3.5 miles

Difficulty: Variable—the hike up East Branch Mill Creek is moderate, the hike along Middle Branch Trail is easy, and the hike down Middle Branch Mill Creek is very difficult for the first .25 mile but then becomes moderate; numerous stream crossings; extensive off-trail hiking and bushwhacking; terrain along waterfalls is steep, rocky, and eroded; do not attempt during high water or icy conditions

Highlights: Several beautiful waterfalls, wildlife, scenic mountain streams

Elevation change: 450 feet

Directions: From US 220/I-180, take the Montoursville exit and follow PA 87 north. After about 23 miles, you reach the small town of Hillsgrove. Mill Creek Road, a dirt road, is to your left about .4 mile north of the Hillsgrove Hotel. Mill Creek Road is the left turn immediately after the small bridge that crosses Mill Creek. Follow Mill Creek Road past Big Hollow Road to your left, a hunting camp, and Camels Road to your right. About 4.2 miles from PA 87, a small gravel parking lot is on your left, just before the bridge that crosses Mill Creek, a good trout stream.

M ost hikers spend their time in Wyoming State Forest's beautiful eastern section, which harbors Loyalsock Trail and numerous other trails and scenic areas. However, the state forest's isolated western section is also worthy of your attention, despite its lack of a cohesive trail system. Here you will find spectacular Hoagland Vista as it overlooks the Hoagland Branch Gorge, Bearwallow Pond, and the numerous cascades, flumes, and pools along the Hoagland Branch. If you're willing to bushwhack, there are also several waterfalls.

Begin by crossing the bridge and bushwhacking to your right up Mill Creek. A hunting cabin is off to your left. Mill Creek babbles over a cobblestone bed underneath a grove of hemlocks. After .2 mile, East Branch and Middle Branch join each other; bushwhack up East Branch, the small stream to your right. The terrain is moderate as you hike upstream, and crossing the stream at normal levels is not difficult. I generally found myself hiking up along the right (east) bank, but you will have to cross the stream when one bank becomes too steep. The banks close in on the stream, creating a short gorge, but there is room to hike along the right bank. A few hundred feet farther, the stream bends right and hides East Branch Falls, a 25-foot waterfall. Climb up the steep bank to the top, and you are rewarded with a small chasm hiding flumes, whirlpools, and another waterfall with twin leaps. The erosional features are excellent as the stream has carved down into the fractured bedrock.

Take a moment to orient yourself. Walker Road is only 100 feet to your right; to complete the loop,

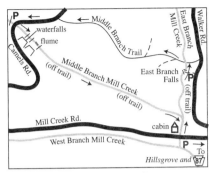

Hike 33: Middle Branch Trail

you need to find Middle Branch Trail, the only blazed trail on this hike. The trail is a few hundred feet upstream and is blazed red; it follows an old, grassy forest road. You can also walk up Walker Road to intersect the trail. Turn left onto the trail and bear right at a Y with another old forest road. You gradually climb to the top of the plateau, passing a young hardwood forest with numerous glades. The trail bears left and joins a wide, grassy forest road. There are numerous glades nearby, offering a great opportunity to see wildlife and wildflowers. The trail is level and rock free. After .25 mile, the trail narrows a little and becomes more brushy as in enters a mature hardwood forest. You pass a meadow to your left and several seep springs, making sections of this trail wet. Once you reach Camels Road, turn left. Walk down this road for .25 mile until you reach Middle Branch.

Turn left and bushwhack downstream along Middle Branch. At first, the stream babbles over cobblestones, but its character changes once it drops over a 30-foot waterfall into a tight gorge. The stream then drops over a second waterfall about 25 feet high; scramble down between the ledges to the left of the falls. Your fun is not over. The stream drops over a cascade and spirals down a long flume before reaching a 10-foot waterfall and its large pool. This section is very difficult; you must hike along the flume to the left, cross the stream above the 10-foot falls, and scramble down the steep bank to the right of the stream. The terrain is very slippery and difficult. This entire section is rugged, with rock faces and ledges; the only way to see the waterfalls and flumes is to bushwhack along the stream.

After passing the pool, the rocky terrain becomes much more manageable. Simply follow Middle Branch downstream underneath hardwoods. You are treated to another flume, and the stream begins to braid. A small seasonal tributary descends from the left, and hemlocks become more prevalent ahead. Cross the stream whenever you need to. The stream slides down another flume, beneath a ledge with dripping springs on the right bank. Brush begins to dominate the left bank, so it may be easier to hike down the right bank. You reach the juncture with the East Branch and the end of the loop. Retrace your steps to your car.

Worlds End State Park

Despite its small size, Worlds End is one of Pennsylvania's most beautiful state parks. It features waterfalls, white water, rock formations, and spectacular overlooks and vistas. Looking from the scenic Loyalsock Creek to the tops of the surrounding mountains, one cannot help but be captured by the beauty of this park. One of the park's greatest characteristics is its isolation; it is tucked away in a deep canyon far away from the cities and suburbs. Despite this, Worlds End is a very popular park. On any given summer weekend, the parking lot will probably be crowded with visitors; I once counted cars from 10 different states. Unlike most state parks, which have one or two trails with any scenic value, every trail at Worlds End is worth hiking; beauty encompasses the entire park.

All the seasons are equally beautiful at Worlds End. In the spring, the Loyalsock Creek and waterfalls are at their highest. The mountain laurel blooms in June, making Canyon Vista an ideal destination. By mid-October, fall foliage sweeps through the park. And in winter, Worlds End is engulfed in a frozen, desolate tranquility.

This park's greatest feature is the Loyalsock Canyon. Loyalsock Creek has flowed through the Sullivan Highlands for millions of years and has eroded 800 feet of rock to create the canyon that exists today. In choosing its course, the creek flows among rocks having the highest fracture densities and structural weaknesses— in other words, the path of least resistance. As a result, the creek has carved an S curve through its gorge.

Worlds End's unusual name originates from early travelers who used a narrow mountain road on the west side of the creek that made a sharp bend near a cliff above the creek. To these travelers, this was a place to end it all, or it appeared to be the end of the world. The park was also once known as "Whirl's End."

To reach Worlds End State Park, take Route 87 north from the Williamsport area. Turn right onto PA 154 at Forksville; the park is 2 miles farther. On US 220, turn onto PA 154 just outside of Laporte; the park is 7 miles farther.

Contact information: Worlds End State Park, PO Box 62, Forksville, PA 18616-0062; phone: 570-924-3287; website: www.dcnr.state.pa.us/ stateparks; e-mail: worldsendsp@state.pa.us

---

👣 34. Butternut Trail

Duration: 1¹/₂ hours

Distance: 1.5 miles

Difficulty: Easy to moderate—rocky, steep switchback; small stream and spring crossings; steep drop-offs near the trail

Highlights: Vista, glades, small stream with cascades and waterfalls, wildflowers

Elevation change: 400 feet

Directions: The best way to reach the trailhead is to turn into the main parking lot near the bathing area. Drive to the far end of the parking lot, take the road past the concession stand, and cross the bridge. Once you cross the Loyalsock, there is a small parking area to your left; park there. You will see a sign for Butternut Trail.

This trail was established by Ruth Rode, a longtime member of the Alpine Club of Williamsport. The Butternut's trailhead is to the right of the High Rock Trail (Hike No. 35), and the trail is blazed maroon. At first, the trail is somewhat steep as it makes a quick ascent, but it levels off and arrives at a small gravel parking lot and Picnic Area No. 3. Here, the trail makes a left onto an old, narrow jeep road that makes a gradual incline. You then come to an old sign that reads "Upper Road," which is the jeep road to the left, and "Lower Road," which is actually a trail to your right. Make a right onto the trail. At first, the trail makes a moderate incline through a hardwood forest, but it soon follows a gradual decline to Butternut Run. You pass several springs, and to your right is a steep decline that goes all the way down to Loyalsock Creek, which you can both see and hear.

The trail reaches Butternut Run, a small, seasonal stream with numerous cascades and a waterfall about 20 feet high. It is hard to get a good look at the waterfall because the trail traverses the bank above the falls. There are more waterfalls, off the trail, as the run approaches Loyalsock Creek. Cross the run as best you can; there is no bridge. The trail continues to ascend and becomes much rockier. You soon reach a talus slope interspersed with trees; the trail follows steep switchbacks through this rocky area. After several switchbacks, you see a sign telling you to make a left if you want to return to Worlds End or a right if you want to see the vista. Make the right; the vista is a short distance farther.

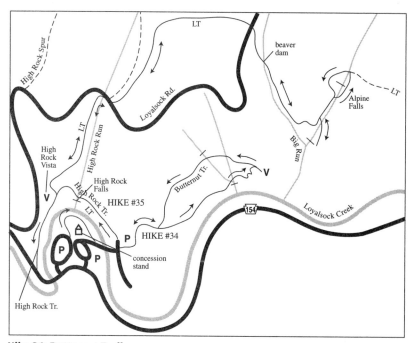

Hike 34: Butternut Trail
Hike 35: High Rock Trail and Alpine Falls

This vista is man-made, created by cutting trees down the mountainside. It offers a nice view of the Loyalsock as it makes a gradual curve into the park. Canyon Vista (Hike No. 36) can be seen off to your left.

To return, retrace your steps back to the sign, and go straight toward Worlds End. Here, the trail is relatively level and crosses Butternut Run, where there are several large cascades. You soon pass an interesting natural feature—a delicate spring-fed waterfall about 30 feet high—about 100 feet to your right. This spring falls over a ledge, and by the time it reaches the trail, it disappears back into the ground. This waterfall is best viewed during periods of sufficient rain.

The trail soon passes through several glades; the first offers a limited view to the southeast. These glades provide habitat for white-tailed deer and several species of wildflowers, such as wild phlox and white and purple violets. The trail also passes by several springs and through even more glades. You then come upon a third sign that points to Worlds End to the left and Loyalsock Trail (LT) to the right. Follow the trail to Worlds End. The trail begins a modest descent, and you come upon the "Upper Road/Lower Road" sign. Follow the jeep road back to the picnic area and to the trailhead.

Butternut Trail is probably the least hiked trail in the park. Its beauty is underestimated, and it can offer you wonderful solitude.

35. High Rock Trail and Alpine Falls

Duration: 5 hours

Distance: 8 miles

Difficulty: Difficult—exceptionally steep, slippery, and rocky in parts; precipitous cliffs and banks; several stream crossings

Highlights: Vista, waterfalls, High Rock, white water, scenic mountain streams

Elevation change: 850 feet

Directions: From Forksville, take PA 154 into Worlds End. The main parking area is to your left once you cross Loyalsock Creek; park there. From US 220, take PA 154 into the park. Turn right into the main parking area before you cross the Loyalsock.

Even though it is short, High Rock Trail is difficult because it is both steep and rocky. It is also a scenic hike and allows you to overlook Loyalsock Canyon. The trail is blazed yellow; the first half of the hike also has blazes for the Loyalsock Trail (LT). From High Rock Vista, this hike follows the LT about 3.5 miles to Alpine Falls.

To begin, you can walk along the bank of the Loyalsock away from the bridge and the swimming area, or you can walk along the paved road up to the concession stand and make a left onto High Rock Trail, which goes down to and along the Loyalsock. If you decide to hike along the bank, you will pass picnic tables and pavilions; if the creek is low, you can hike along the rocky shore of the Loyalsock. You can also see close-up the rapids that make the Loyalsock famous. This route soon intercepts High Rock Trail. If you choose to take High Rock Trail, proceed to the left of the concession stand, where you pass a memorial, water pump, and picnic pavilion. The trail then brings you close to the Loyalsock. Across the creek is High Rock, a sheer, colorful rock face that is about 100 feet high. The Loyalsock flows up against High Rock as it begins to make its S curve. During periods of plentiful rain, a faint waterfalls drops from High Rock directly into the Loyalsock. These waterfalls become cascading rainbows when the sunlight hits them right. And in winter, these waterfalls create impressive columns of ice. If you hike upstream along High Rock Trail, you will see High Rock Falls, Worlds End's most impressive waterfall. It is best to view High Rock Falls during the autumn, winter, or spring, because the trees hide the falls in summer, and the waterfall is reduced to a trickle. During periods of rain, however, High Rock Falls is a beautiful 80-foot cascade as it tumbles into the Loyalsock. Enjoy the waterfall now, because you will not have a good view of it when the trail passes above it on the other side of the Loyalsock.

If you hike here in the summer, you may see stacks of stones creating interesting "sculptures" in the Loyalsock's large cobblestone bed. Over the past few years, campers have begun the tradition of stacking stones in these formations. You may also see stones stacked below the swimming dam, along PA 154.

The trail eventually bears to the right away from the Loyalsock to join a paved park road. Follow the road across the bridge, where there is a small picnic and parking area to your left. There you will see a sign pointing to High Rock Trail; to the right is Butternut Trail (Hike No. 34). It is here that your fun begins. The trail makes a gradual incline up the side of Loyalsock Canyon, with some steeper sections. The trail crosses High Rock Run, but you can see only the crest of High Rock Falls. From High Rock Run to High Rock Vista, the trail is almost treacherous because it is incredibly rocky and steep. In fact, there is no actual trail here; you have to follow the blazes up the rock slide. It is very important that you take your time when negotiating this section of the trail. At the top, you reach a hemlock forest and huge boulders. Follow the yellow blazes and the blazes for the LT to reach High Rock Vista, which offers a nice view of the Loyalsock and the picnic area. Do not venture beyond the wooden fence, because there is an almost vertical drop from the vista to Loyalsock Creek. From here, you can also see Canyon Vista, which rises prominently to the southeast. To reach Alpine Falls, follow the LT as it leaves High Rock Trail at the vista; it makes a sharp right and ascends the mountain. If you want to hike only High Rock Trail, simply follow the yellow blazes down to PA 154.

The LT winds around some large boulders, picks up an old forest road, and begins to make a long ascent up High Rock Run. At first, the run is fairly deep in its small glen; however, the LT and the run soon meet. This scenic stream has numerous cascades as it flows around rocks and over small ledges. There are even two small waterfalls about 3 to 5 feet in height. Near the top, hemlocks are numerous, and the trail is often wet.

The LT reaches Loyalsock Road, where you turn right. The trail leaves the road at a small parking area where High Rock Spur (a jeep trail) meets the road. The LT enters a mixed hemlock and hardwood forest and parallels High Rock Spur, which is about 100 to 200 feet off to your left. The LT then makes a sharp right on an old, abandoned forest road. Extensive sections of this trail can be wet. The trail often avoids the road by staying on the bank; other times, you have no choice but to walk through it. It was during this portion of the hike that I saw the most wildlife, including rabbits, squirrels, and chipmunks, as well as several hawks overhead. The trail crosses a couple of springs and begins to make a short descent to Loyalsock Road. The LT crosses the road and continues its gradual descent to Big Run. You reach a beaver dam and its accompanying bog. The LT follows Big Run downstream, crosses it, and makes a right onto an old railroad grade. The grade is level and passes a couple of campsites. To your right, Big Run has carved a deep gorge. The babbling of streams is a common sound along this hike. At the end of the grade, you reach Ken's Window, which offers a limited view of the gorge. The LT continues its ascent through a beautiful hemlock and pine forest and then makes a sharp descent to Tom's Run. At the bottom of the descent, the LT makes a left onto another railroad grade. Follow the grade up Tom's Run and past another campsite.

Here, the LT climbs a steep bank to the left and crosses above Alpine Falls. The red X trail goes up and into Alpine Falls' rocky glen and scrambles alongside the falls. Do not use this trail during heavy rain or if it is icy. Alpine Falls has carved a beautiful glen of fractured rock with numerous overhangs. The falls itself bounces down numerous ledges and is about 25 to 30 feet high. Above Alpine Falls is another waterfall about 6 feet high. There are a couple of campsites at the top of the falls. This is an ideal place for a break. When you are ready, follow the LT back down.

Once you have made it back down to the grade via the LT, there is another waterfall you may wish to see. Below the grade and along Tom's Run is a campsite, the first one you passed upon entering Tom's Run. Across the run is another discernible grade. Follow the grade down a few hundred feet until you reach the state forest boundary (marked by white blazes on the trees and a "No Trespassing" sign). To your right is a 15- to 20-foot waterfall that flows down a narrow rock crevasse. From here, Tom's Run joins Big Run, which continues to tumble its way down to Loyalsock Creek. Unfortunately, it isn't possible to hike any farther. From here, retrace your steps all the way back to High Rock Vista.

Back at High Rock Vista, follow High Rock Trail to the right as it makes a steep descent. The trail is on the edge of a steep bank that drops off into Loyalsock Creek. The trail swerves to the right, away from the steep bank, and descends to PA 154, where you make a left. Follow PA 154 across the bridge and to the parking area, which is also to your left.

36. Canyon Vista

Duration: 2¹/₂ to 3 hours

Distance: 2 miles

Difficulty: Difficult—rocky, steep, and slippery in sections

Highlights: One of Pennsylvania's most famous vistas, rock formations, scenic stream with several small waterfalls and flumes

Elevation change: 700 feet

Directions: From Forksville, take PA 154 into the park. Drive past the main parking area and the park office. Drive past Double Run Road to your right; the parking area for this hike is on the right a few hundred feet farther. There is a sign for the Double Run Nature Trail.

This route to Canyon Vista is a hiker's delight and is the most popular and beautiful trail at Worlds End. Please note that there is a trail at Worlds End named Canyon Vista Trail. The route described here uses only a small portion of that trail. I suggest that you use this route, because it is far more scenic than hiking Canyon Vista Trail in its entirety.

Your ascent to Canyon Vista begins by taking the white- and green-blazed Double Run Nature Trail from the small parking lot along PA 154. The trail is level and well defined and closely parallels Double Run, a crystal-clear stream. After about 800 feet, the trail is very close to the run, and you can see a small waterfall and flume to your right. A short distance farther, the West Branch joins Double Run—do not cross either stream. Stay on the left bank of Double Run, and you will see the red and yellow blazes of the Link and Loyalsock Trails. Follow these blazes up a small embankment, where the two trails separate— the Loyalsock (LT) to the left, and the Link to the right. Follow the

Link Trail. Here the trail is above Double Run, but it slowly descends and brings you very close to it. The trail always stays to the left of Double Run, and because it is so close to the run, it can be slippery. Here the trail squeezes between massive boulders and up steep banks as it follows Double Run upstream. Double Run is a stream of exceptional beauty, and the scenery is excellent. Massive boulders litter the streambed, and the run has even carved itself into solid rock. You can see several small waterfalls, flumes, deep pools, and cascades. The trail scrambles over some more boulders and up the bank, where there is a log bench with a nice view down the run.

The trail then turns away from Double Run and crosses Mineral Spring Road. Although the trail is steep and nearly overgrown here, the ascent to Canyon Vista is not too difficult. The trail curves around a ledge, levels off, and soon joins the blue-blazed Canyon Vista Trail; follow both Link and Canyon Vista Trails to Canyon Vista. Here the trail makes its gradual climb up the mountainside to Canyon Vista. The trail is narrow and eroded in places; be careful, because there is a steep drop to your left. The trail soon reaches the top and wanders through a beautiful hemlock grove that offers broken views through the forest canopy. A little farther is the famous Canyon Vista. At 1,750 feet, Canyon Vista is not very high, but it offers incredible mountain scenery and an awesome view of Loyalsock Canyon. From here, you can see the Loyalsock's S curve as it winds through Worlds End; Double Run gorge, where you just hiked from, is also clearly visible. Even at this height, both the Loyalsock and Double Run are audible. This view is especially notable in June when the mountain laurel blooms and in October during the height of the autumn foliage. Across Cold Run Road is the Rock Garden, a collection of massive sandstone boulders with narrow passageways in between them.

After you have enjoyed the vista, follow the blue-blazed Canyon Vista Trail in the opposite direction from which you came. The trail weaves through a young, regenerating forest with many saplings. Here, the trail stays fairly level as it circumvents the mountainside, but it is very rocky with a lot of root entanglements. There is a steep drop-off to your left. The trail widens and enters a blowdown area with thickets of weeds and bushes. Once you reenter the forest, the trail descends into a gully and intersects with the LT. Turn left onto the LT, which makes a sharp, eroded descent along the gully of a small, seasonal stream; it is important that you exercise caution during this portion of the trail. The trail begins to level out as it turns to the left and

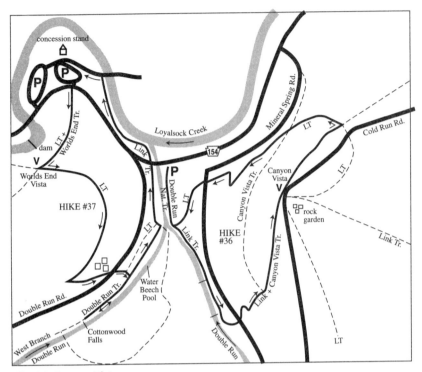

Hike 36: Canyon Vista
Hike 37: Worlds End Vista and Cottonwood Falls

wraps around the base of the mountain in front of Canyon Vista. Here the forest is somewhat sparse, with a thick understory of vegetation nourished by several springs. The LT then crosses Canyon Vista Trail; continue on the LT. The trail makes a slight descent and enters an extremely rocky slope with hemlocks. Here the trail is not discernible as it crosses boulders and more rocks than you can imagine; as a result, you need to pay special attention to the blazes. The trail makes a switchback down the rocky slope and crosses Mineral Spring Road. Once you cross the road, the trail is level and relatively rock free as it descends to the Link Trail and Double Run. From here, return the way you came by following the green- and white-blazed Double Run Nature Trail back to PA 154.

37. Worlds End Vista and Cottonwood Falls

Duration:	1¹/₂ to 2 hours

Distance: 2 miles

Difficulty: Moderate—the beginning is steep; rocky, eroded, and rugged along the West Branch of Double Run; scramble over ledges right along Loyalsock Creek

Highlights: Vista, Cottonwood Falls, rock formations, numerous small waterfalls and flumes, hiking along Loyalsock Creek

Elevation change: 400 feet

Directions: Park at the park office parking lot. The hike both begins and ends there.

This relatively short hike is scenic and showcases the splendor of Worlds End. It uses portions of the Loyalsock Trail (LT), Worlds End Trail, Double Run Nature Trail, and Link Trail—creating a loop that relatively few people hike.

The LT passes in front of the park office, which houses a small nature shop, maps, stuffed specimens of regional wildlife, and scenic pictures of the area. The LT crosses PA 154 and passes through a picnic grove; here the trail is level. You will notice that the trail is also blazed yellow for Worlds End Trail. Once the trail leaves the picnic area, it makes an increasingly steep ascent through a hemlock forest. There are broken views of the canyon through the trees to your right. After about .2 mile, the trail begins to level and arrives at Worlds End Vista. The view is a narrow window through the hemlocks looking almost directly down on the swimming area, the PA 154 bridge, and Loyalsock Creek as it flows from High Rock.

Continue to follow the trail, and you soon reach Pioneer Road. This road once connected Eagles Mere to Forksville. It was abandoned in 1895, when an easier route was established along the Loyalsock. Here the LT and Worlds End Trail split; the LT makes a sharp left onto Pioneer Road, while Worlds End Trail crosses it and continues to ascend the mountain. Follow the LT. Here the trail is level, marking the end of any serious climbing for the remainder of the hike. The LT leaves the hemlock forest and enters an area with lots of briers and brush, offering broken views of the canyon to your left. Here the deciduous forest was defoliated by insects, which resulted in a high mortality rate. Sunlight was able to reach the forest floor, causing the explosive growth of brier bushes, which almost choke out the trail. Many trails in the area have the same problem. Eventually, the trail enters a mixed hemlock and hardwood forest, and the briers relent. The trail crosses several springs and a few blowdowns. It was here that three deer kept running away from me whenever I approached as I hiked down the trail.

The LT makes a sharp left, leaving Pioneer Road, and makes a gradual descent to Double Run Road. As you near the road, look to your left and notice the massive boulders. Follow the LT as it crosses Double Run Road. After you cross the road, there is an important shortcut you should take. The LT makes a slight descent once it crosses the road, and about 20 feet from the road on the LT, there is a shortcut trail to your right; take it. After about 100 feet, this trail meets the green- and white-blazed Double Run Nature Trail. If you don't take this shortcut, you will hike down the LT for about .25 mile, only to come back up the same way on Double Run Nature Trail. Turn right on Double Run Trail. All along the creek, this trail is slippery, rocky, and eroded, so be careful. The West Branch of Double Run is very scenic, with its deep pools, flumes, small waterfalls, and Cottonwood Falls, at which you soon arrive. Cottonwood Falls is not a large waterfall; it's not even 20 feet high. However, it is a powerful waterfall, and this power has created its most impressive feature—a surprisingly large, deep pool. On the far side of the stream, several springs tumble into the pool. A short distance above Cottonwood Falls is another pretty waterfall, about 5 feet high. I once met a hiker on this trail who told me that there is another waterfall above Cottonwood that is even higher, but I've never been able to find it.

To continue, retrace your steps on Double Run Trail, following the West Branch of Double Run downstream. The trail passes many small scenic waterfalls and flumes. There is one narrow waterfall about 3 feet high that forms a broad flume across a rock face. You pass two pools, one of which is Water Beech Pool, a deep pool fed by a 4-foot waterfall. The trail then traverses the edge of a steep bank above the stream; be especially careful here. The trail arrives where West Branch and Double Run meet. Do not follow Double Run Trail, which crosses both streams and heads toward the small parking lot on PA 154. Instead, turn left onto Link Trail, which heads downstream on the left bank of Double Run. This is also where the LT enters; you would've had to hike all the way down here if you hadn't taken that previous shortcut. Link Trail crosses PA 154 and crosses the floodplain to Loyalsock Creek. If the Loyalsock is too high, you will have to walk along PA 154. The trail stays close to the creek and crosses a stone causeway to a series of stone ledges that border a deep pool within the Loyalsock. This is an ideal spot to take a rest and enjoy the scenery. From here, you can see Canyon Vista rising prominently to the southeast. This is also a good place for wildflowers. There are several names carved into the ledges, one dating back to 1906. The trail scrambles across these ledges, reenters the rocky floodplain, and ends at the paved road and bridge that access the cabin area. Turn left onto the road and go up to the concession stand and the park office parking area.

Tiadaghton State Forest
(Eastern Section)

Covering about 215,000 acres, Tiadaghton State Forest is the third largest in Pennsylvania. This guide covers hikes in Tiadaghton's spectacular eastern section, which is wild, remote, and exceptionally beautiful. The McIntyre Wild Area contains the watersheds of four streams cascading in numerous waterfalls. Rock Run is considered Pennsylvania's most beautiful stream, and it has carved itself into solid bedrock to create chasms, waterfalls, flumes, and pools. Sharp Top Vista is utterly astonishing as it looks over a wide, wooded valley. These are just a few of the gems this region contains. Also, there are numerous ghost towns in this state forest—remnants from the heydays of the logging and mining era—so you may never be truly alone on your hikes.

Contact information: Tiadaghton State Forest, 423 East Central Avenue, South Williamsport, PA 17702; phone: 570-327-3450; website: www.dcnr. state.pa.us/forestry; e-mail: fd12@state.pa.us

38. Sandy Bottom

Duration:	1 to 2 hours

Distance: 3.8 miles

Difficulty: Easy—level, broad, and sandy. Difficult if you decide to climb to the vistas; unblazed trail becomes rocky and steeper; bushwhacking required

Highlights: Diverse forest, trout fishing, Loyalsock Creek, vistas, rock outcrops

Elevation change: 400 feet

Directions: The entrance to Sandy Bottom is easy to miss. It is on the left along PA 87, about 17.4 miles from the Montoursville exit on US 220/ I-180, or 2.3 miles north of Barbours. There is a small sign along the road. Sandy Bottom is about 5.6 miles south of Hillsgrove. At the entrance, follow the narrow dirt road a short distance down to the parking area.

Sandy Bottom is typically a trout fisherman's destination, as it features special-regulation waters along this stretch of the Loyalsock. So expect company, especially in April or May.

Sandy Bottom first attracted my attention when I was driving along PA 87 and saw a sign indicating that there was a nature trail here. Unfortunately, there is little evidence of a nature trail, except for intermittent, faded orange blazes and one numbered station, which appears to have been randomly placed. There are plans to rebuild the nature trail.

From the parking area, pass around the gate and follow the forest road. Off to the left is a large riparian island, and on the far side of the island is the Loyalsock. The trail passes through a hardwood forest dominated by maple, oak, hickory, and beech trees. A few hundred feet farther, the trail enters an area with numerous hemlock and pine trees. Soon you see the Loyalsock, which is the size of a small river. On the other side is a steep mountainside, giving this hike an isolated feel. Here the Loyalsock flows against the steep, crescent-shaped flank of Scaife Knob, which rises 1,100 feet above where you are hiking.

This short section where the trail is parallel to the Loyalsock is the most scenic. The creek is wide, clear, and beautiful and contains numerous islands. This is a great place to fish. In spring, trout prevails. By summer, the warmer water becomes home to smallmouth bass. High above the creek are rock ledges and outcrops. To the right of the trail is a thick, mysterious plantation of red pine. Soon the trail leaves the creek and passes a plantation of white pine. After a short distance, the trail comes to a Y, where an old forest road continues straight, and another road comes in sharply from the right; this marks your turnaround point.

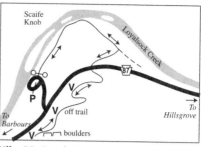

Hike 38: Sandy Bottom

If you'd like to extend your hike to see the many rock outcrops and vistas on the other side of PA 87, make the sharp right turn at the Y. This old forest road is unblazed, and this segment of the hike requires bushwhacking and off-trail hiking. Climb the old road up to PA 87. At the highway, there is an eroded forest grade diagonally across PA 87 to your left. It is initially hard to see, but once you enter the forest, it becomes more noticeable. This unblazed grade proceeds straight for a few hundred feet, turns right, ascends, and then turns left as it reaches level ground. A few hundred feet to your right are exposed ledges offering views of the Loyalsock. The grade begins a mild ascent and turns left at the base of a talus slope. Once again it ascends and levels off among hemlocks and mountain laurel. The grade becomes imperceptible as it turns right and tunnels through thick stands of laurel. There may be pieces of fluorescent tape tied to twigs and branches. The level grade traverses the edge of the plateau, passing more ledges and vistas of the valley below.

The grade now completely disappears. Follow the edge of the plateau until you reach a saddle. The laurel thins out, and hardwoods become more prevalent. To your right are exposed ledges and boulders. Keep the same elevation as you hike across the saddle and reenter the hemlocks among masses of jumbled boulders. Begin to ascend to your left over the boulders, and you once again reach the edge of the plateau. Massive boulders dominate, with one round boulder cracked like an egg. Negotiate this difficult terrain carefully to reach the last exposed ledge, which offers an excellent panorama of the twisting Loyalsock and its valley. A massive boulder is behind this vista. Return the way you came.

Back at the parking area, notice a small grove of sizable hemlocks downstream, or just south, of the parking area. Many of these trees have had their roots exposed from flooding, even though they are several feet above the creek. Here, the Loyalsock curves around the large riparian island discussed previously and bounces over some riffles into a scenic pool. In warm weather, you may want to go off the trail and explore the numerous islands and the rocky shores of the creek.

39. Allegheny Ridge

Duration: 4 hours

Distance: 6.2 miles

Difficulty: Difficult—the climb to Sock Rock is rocky, steep, and eroded in places; the descent through Pete's Hollow is steep in places, rocky, and follows the bed of an intermittent stream

Highlights: Views, mountain laurel

Elevation change: 1,100 feet

Directions: Proceeding north on PA 87 from Montoursville, turn right on Little Bear Road, which is about 9.3 miles from the Montoursville exit of US 220/I-180. Follow Little Bear Road for about .75 mile until you reach the forest headquarters on your right across the creek. There are some parking spaces there. Proceeding south on PA 87, Little Bear Road is almost 6 miles from Barbours.

This hike marks the beginning of the famed Loyalsock Trail (LT). From forest headquarters, walk down Little Bear Road toward PA 87. Off to your left is Little Bear Creek, which has a few deep manmade pools harboring trout. You also pass a sign for a hike to Smiths Knob (Hike No. 40). Upon reaching PA 87, turn left and hike for about .75 mile to the LT trailhead. The hike along this busy highway is not ideal, but it's necessary to complete the loop, so it's best to get it out of the way first. If you are determined to avoid this roadside walk, I describe an alternative later.

Upon reaching the LT's trailhead, climb the trail up a steep bank. Soon you turn right onto an old woods road. This level section doesn't last long before you have to turn left and ascend the mountain. The trail is steep, eroded, and rocky and passes between ledges. After leveling off some, the trail continues to ascend via switchbacks and passes a view to your right of the Loyalsock Valley. The trail becomes increasingly rocky as you ascend. Soon you pass Sock Rock, a large, flat, oval-shaped boulder that is rather inconspicuous. The trail continues its rocky ascent before it reaches the top of the plateau.

Upon reaching the top, the trail's character changes dramatically; it's level and gentle as it passes through mountain laurel, thickets of pine, and a canopy dominated by oak. This area is known as Laurel Flat. After .75 mile, you reach a grassy forest road, which also serves as a bridle trail. To the left, this trail also marks the beginning of red X-1 (RX-1), a connector trail that meets the LT near the top of Pete's Hollow and can be a return route if you parked at the LT trailhead and want to avoid the walk along PA 87. Alternatively, you can park at forest headquarters, hike up the LT in Pete's Hollow, and use RX-1 and the LT as a loop. The LT turns left and stays on the forest road as it crosses a few small springs and begins a gentle ascent to the Allegheny Ridge, also known as the Allegheny Front. Follow the LT as it turns left off the road. The trail burrows through the laurel and passes underneath an oak forest. The LT makes a gradual, rocky ascent before reaching the edge of the Allegheny Ridge. You are soon treated to a few broken views through the canopy. The trail makes a gradual descent and passes

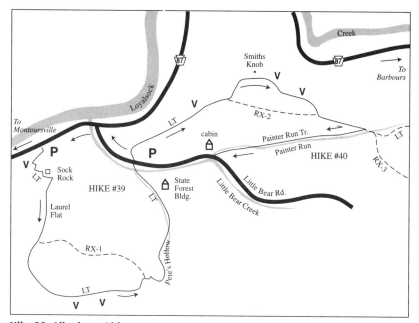

Hike 39: Allegheny Ridge
Hike 40: Smiths Knob and Painter Run

another RX trail—a connector trail to RX-1. After making another gradual climb, the LT presents numerous broken views of the farmlands below as it traverses the edge of the Allegheny Ridge, sometimes passing above small cliffs. There are two nice views cut into the canopy, with the second being the most expansive. The gentle hills, contoured farm fields, and woodlots are scenic any time of year, but I recommend that you hike this section when there are no leaves on the trees for views that are continuous and expansive.

After making a descent, you once again reach the bridle trail–grassy forest road and RX-1. If you parked at the LT's trailhead along PA 87, you may want to use RX-1 to return to your car. Otherwise, proceed on the LT as it makes a gradual descent and turns left off the bridle trail. Here, the trail begins its rapid descent down Pete's Hollow. The LT actually uses the bed of an intermittent stream as it passes through a scenic forest of some large specimens of hemlock and pine. The trail is often rocky and steep. Near the bottom of the hollow, you pass through an area that appears to have been blown down in a windstorm; notice a large sandstone bluff off to your right. The trail crosses a stream and follows an old woods road, called Peter's Path, as it makes its final descent through hemlocks to forest headquarters.

40. Smiths Knob and Painter Run

Duration: 3¹/₂ to 4 hours

Distance: 5.7 miles

Difficulty: Difficult—long ascent to Smiths Knob, where the trail passes above cliffs; some sections are eroded and steep; bushwhacking and off-trail hiking necessary

Highlights: Vistas from Smiths Knob, Painter Run

Elevation change: 1,100 feet

Directions: Proceeding north on PA 87, turn right on Little Bear Road, which is about 9.3 miles from the Montoursville exit of US 220/I-180. Follow Little Bear Road for about .75 mile until you reach the forest headquarters on your right across the creek. There are some parking spaces there. Proceeding south on PA 87, Little Bear Road is almost 6 miles from Barbours.

Smiths Knob is notable for its round, distinctive peak—a geologic anomaly among the plateaus that dominate the region. From your car along Little Bear Creek near the ranger station, head down Little

Bear Road, following the Loyalsock Trial (LT) blazes. Soon the trail leaves the road and scampers up the bank to the right and passes a register. Here the trail begins its long ascent to Smiths Knob. At first, the trail is steep, but it soon becomes more gradual. The hardwood forest is open, with a thick understory of striped maple. Even in the summer, you can see deep into the woods. Following an old forest road, you approach the ridgeline high above the Loyalsock. You soon pass two scenic vistas of the Loyalsock far below.

The trail levels off before it makes a final, steep climb up Smiths Knob. At first, the ascent is rocky and eroded. The climb reaches a narrow, grassy flank and you can peer down either side into the surrounding forest. You are afforded another nice vista to the south overlooking Painter Run, along which you will soon hike. Upon reaching the top of Smiths Knob, you pass a campsite, and there is a spectacular view of the Loyalsock Valley to the east. Here, you are about 1,100 feet above the Loyalsock. PA 87 appears perfectly straight as it slices through the forest. Please use caution at this vista; the eastern face of Smiths Knob is ringed with cliffs.

After taking a rest, follow the LT as it makes a steep, eroded descent, passing ledges and boulders. To your left are cliffs and incredibly steep terrain. The trail levels and passes DER View, which looks north across the Loyalsock. It is named after the former Department of Environmental Resources, whose employees cut the vista. The trail picks up an old forest road and soon intercepts red X-2 (RX-2). The trail then makes a gradual descent to Painter Run.

Painter Run is a beautiful mountain stream. It tumbles down a small glen across a carpet of moss. Upon reaching the run, turn right and head downstream; there are no signs or blazes, but as you proceed, the trail will become more perceptible. Because the forest is relatively open, with limited undergrowth, the hiking is easy. Pines and hemlocks dominate the bottom portion of the glen along the run, while hardwoods dominate the higher slopes. The trail stays primarily to the right of the run, but you have to cross the run at least three times. You pass numerous pools harboring native brook trout that bolt for cover at the slightest disturbance. The trail gradually resembles an old forest road and crosses a talus slope, under which the run temporarily disappears. You pass a few campsites, and the trail makes a final crossing to the left bank and passes behind a large, tan-colored hunting cabin. Upon reaching Little Bear Road, turn right and follow it about .75 mile to your car.

🚶🚶 41. Rider Park

Duration:	2 hours
Distance:	3 miles
Difficulty:	Easy—gradual inclines and declines; wet and rocky in parts
Highlights:	Views, open fields and meadows
Elevation change:	300 feet

Directions: From PA 87, about 4.5 miles north of the Montoursville exit of US 220/I-180, turn left onto PA 973. Make a right onto SR 2022 at the small town of Warrensville. After about 1.5 miles, Caleb Road is on your right, and there's a small sign for Rider Park. Follow Caleb Road as it ascends the mountain and ends at the park's parking area.

Although it borders Tiadaghton State Forest, Rider Park is a community park and is not a part of the state forest system. Like many community parks, Rider offers an extensive system of trails, creating numerous hiking options. This route takes you to the park's most impressive features—its vistas. From the small parking area, take the yellow-blazed Katy Jane Trail as it follows a narrow, old forest road. At first, the trail is level, but it begins a gradual ascent as it climbs the ridge. You reach a vista looking out to the east, with Smiths Knob rising prominently. This vista is partially overgrown with brush, so it is best seen when the leaves are off the trees.

At this first vista, the trail takes a sharp right and makes another quick ascent to the ridgeline. Hike along the top of the ridge, with crumbling ledges to your right. The topography of this trail reminds me of the Appalachian Trail in Berks County, where it traverses the top of Blue Mountain. The trail begins a gradual descent and bears left, where it reaches another vista providing a scenic view of the farmlands of Lycoming County. Off to the southeast flows Loyalsock Creek, and Bald Eagle Mountain rises to the south. Although Williamsport is only about 6 or 7 miles to the south, it cannot be seen thanks to the hilly farmlands.

The trail continues its gradual descent until it reaches a juncture with the blue-blazed Saddle Trail. You can continue straight on Katy Jane Trail as it follows the ridgeline and makes a half loop back to the park road, where you turn right to return to the parking area. Or you

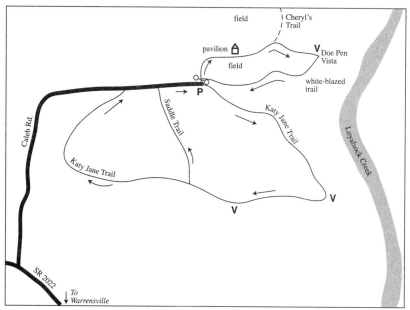

Hike 41: Rider Park

can take Saddle Trail down to the park road, where you also turn right to return to the parking area.

Once you return to the parking area, hike the gated park access road to the pavilion and Doe Pen Vista through fields and meadows that are slowly reverting to woodlands. The grassy road bears right through the open fields and passes the pavilion. It makes a gradual descent and enters the forest. Right before you see a sign for Cheryl's Trail, there is an unmarked trail to your right with a small, distant sign indicating "vista." Follow this trail a short distance to Doe Pen Vista. This vista overlooks the Loyalsock Valley and is shaded by hemlocks.

To return, follow a white-blazed trail that leaves the vista to the left (south). This trail passes hemlock, pine, and laurel as it traverses the edge of a glen. You cross a small stream, bear right, and enter the field you first hiked through. The pavilion is off to your right. The trail follows the edge of the field, passes several bluebird houses, and soon returns you to the park access road and the parking area.

🚶🚶 42. Sharp Top Vista

Duration:	2 to 3 hours
Distance:	6 miles
Difficulty:	Moderate—gradual ascent and descent; briers may be a problem
Highlights:	Spectacular vista
Elevation change:	750 feet

Directions: From Williamsport, head north on US 15. Take the exit for PA 14 at the village of Trout Run. After about 8 miles, at the tiny village of Marsh Hill, turn right onto Pleasant Stream Road. This road is paved at first but eventually becomes a narrow, but drivable, dirt road. After about 6 miles, you will see small parking areas on both sides of the road; park there. This point is easy to miss, so keep an eye out for the Old Loggers Path (OLP) blazes and the sign for Long Run Trail.

To shorten your hike, this trail can also be accessed via Butternut Trail. Drive almost a mile farther on Pleasant Stream Road, where there is a small parking area. A small sign for Butternut Trail is on your right.

This hike takes you to one of the most astonishing vistas in Pennsylvania. The entire hike follows the orange-blazed OLP, and you have to return the way you came.

From the small parking area on Pleasant Stream Road, follow the old railroad grade upstream (do not follow the OLP along Long Run Trail). At this point, Pleasant Stream is out of sight to your right. The trail is wet in spots, and you may have to circumvent a blowdown. After about .3 mile, Pleasant Stream comes into view as it babbles its way to Lycoming Creek. The trail follows this grade for almost a mile before it turns right; Butternut Trail joins from the left. The trail makes a mild descent and fords Pleasant Stream. Be extremely careful crossing this stream in high water. Despite being a medium-sized stream that diminishes in the summer, Pleasant Stream has a floodplain that is characteristic of a river. Follow the trail as it passes a campsite to your left and bears right, then left to enter Butternut Run's gentle glen.

Now you begin your ascent up Burnetts Ridge to Sharp Top. The trail follows an old woods road on the left side of Butternut Run. The climb is long but not very steep. As you reach the top of the plateau, briers become an increasing problem, and there are extensive areas of

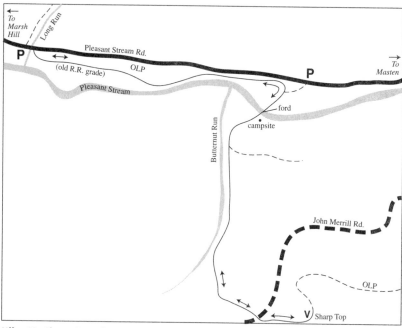

Hike 42: Sharp Top Vista

dead trees, victims of insect infestation or possibly acid rain. It was here that a fawn nearly ran into me as it was following its mother when I was hiking in late spring. The trail crosses a dirt road and turns left to traverse the edge of Burnetts Ridge above small ledges and cliffs.

Follow the trail's mild, rocky ascent as it meets another dirt road, which soon takes you to Sharp Top Vista. This expansive vista overlooks a broad, wooded valley. To the south is a water gap between Cove and Camp Mountains. To the east, you may be able to see the southern face of Burnetts Ridge and Sprout Point. If you look carefully, High Knob Overlook (Hike No. 27) can be seen over Gooseberry Mountain. One of the greatest features of this vista is its isolation; instead of fields, farms, and towns, you are treated to a sylvan spectacle. When it is time to leave, retrace your steps.

If you happen to have the trail map for the OLP, you will notice another vista, Sprout Point, farther to the east. This vista is becoming overgrown by trees and offers only a narrow view, so it is not nearly as breathtaking as Sharp Top.

🥾🥾 43. Sullivan Mountain

Duration:	3 to 4 hours
Distance:	7.7 miles

Difficulty: Moderate—mostly level; some short but steep ascents and descents; rocky and wet in sections

Highlights: Vistas, rock formations, massive boulders

Elevation change: 300 feet

Directions: This is an isolated hike. From Williamsport, take US 15 north toward Mansfield. At Trout Run, follow PA 14 for about 11 miles to the small village of Ralston. Upon entering Ralston, turn right after the Methodist church (which is on your left) onto Thompson Street. The street turns left, then right where it crosses over Lycoming Creek. You are now on Rock Run Road. Follow this road in its entirety; along the way, you pass the trailheads for Hike Nos. 44, 45, and 46. After almost 4.5 miles, the road turns right, crosses Rock Run, and becomes Yellow Dog Road. Follow Yellow Dog Road as it ascends the plateau for about 2 miles. As you reach the top of the plateau, you will see the orange blazes of the Old Loggers Path (OLP) where the road makes a sharp left turn. There are a few spaces to park along the left side of the road.

This beautiful hike utilizes the popular, orange-blazed OLP and features scenic mountain streams, rock formations, and several vistas at the top of Sullivan Mountain.

Because this is a double-loop hike, you can begin by taking either the OLP or Ellenton Ridge Road via Yellow Dog Road; I chose the latter. Walk up Yellow Dog Road for about .5 mile until you reach the point where the road makes a sharp left. This is where Yellow Dog Road ends and Ellenton Ridge Road begins. Turn right and pass the gate. A trail sign indicates that Rock Run Vista is 3.5 miles farther. At one time, this road connected Ellenton to Ralston; however, this section of the road is no longer open to traffic. The unblazed trail follows the wide, level, grassy road as it passes through a hardwood forest with little underbrush. The forest floor is a carpet of ferns.

You pass a juncture with Long Run Trail to the right and a small glade. This same trail descends to the trailhead of the Sharp Top Vista hike (Hike No. 42). Pine, spruce, and hemlock surround the trail. Off to your right, there is a wetland from which Doe Run emerges. The trail continues straight and level. Avoid an obvious forest road to the left where the trail proceeds straight and crosses a pipeline swath, offering a narrow view of the plateau to the north. From here, the trail narrows, but it can still be easily followed. You follow a seasonal streambed through a grove of spruces. Another wetland is off to your left. The trail meets the OLP at a campsite. Although you will eventually return to this point, proceed straight on the OLP and cross Buck Run to see the beautiful vistas on top of Sullivan Mountain.

The trail continues on grassy Ellenton Ridge Road and passes gated Crandalltown Trail to your left. You will return via this trail after climbing to the vistas. About .25 mile farther, the OLP makes a sharp left and begins a rocky, steep ascent. This turn is very easy to miss, so make sure you pay attention to the orange blazes. Fortunately, the ascent is short; it passes underneath boulders and ledges. The OLP bears right upon reaching the top and tunnels through sheep and mountain laurel. There are numerous ledges and large boulders off to your left. The trail traverses the edge of the plateau and reaches the first vista. From here, you have an expansive view of the plateau to the west and north. The gorge carved by Rock Run can be clearly seen, as

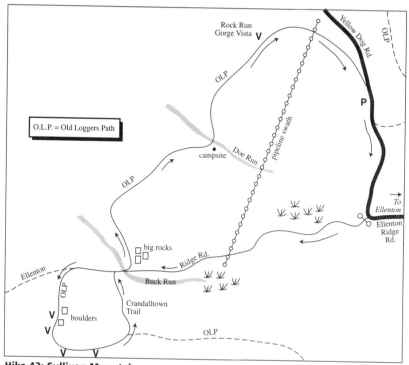

Hike 43: Sullivan Mountain

well as the steep glen carved by Miners Run. Another exposed ledge offers a second vista just a few feet ahead on the trail. Sunsets from these vistas are especially memorable.

The OLP continues along the edge of the plateau, passing more large ledges and boulders, some of them massive. Follow the trail as it makes a mild ascent and veers left through a glade of ferns. You soon reach another vista from a flaking ledge, this one to the south. The view is almost completely undisturbed as you overlook Pleasant Stream's narrow valley. The trail traverses the edge of another ledge, offering another vista, before it turns left at a boulder standing almost upright in between ledges. You are brought to a final vista with a wild view of Sixth Bottom Hollow and the long, deep valley carved by Pleasant Stream. From here, you can return to the point where you first met the OLP, but I suggest you return via the much easier Crandalltown Trail, creating a mini-loop.

Follow the OLP as it rapidly descends between and beneath more ledges and boulders. The trail continues its descent until it makes a sharp right at a large hemlock and a campsite. To your left, an unblazed trail disappears into the forest along an old forest road; this is Crandalltown Trail. Follow this level trail for less than .5 mile, pass the gate, and rejoin the OLP, where you turn right; then cross Buck Run and make a left, following the OLP. It was here you first met the OLP while hiking along Ellenton Ridge Road. Follow the OLP back to your car, parked at Yellow Dog Road.

The trail immediately passes house-sized boulders of conglomerate to your right. Off to your left, Buck Run cascades down to Rock Run. The trail begins a mild descent as it passes through a hardwood forest dominated by maples. You cross several springs and small streams. The forest is open, with little underbrush. After about 1.5 miles, the trail passes campsites and crosses Doe Run, with its small cascades. The OLP follows the bank above Doe Run for a few hundred feet before it veers right and traverses the edge of the plateau, with limited views of Rock Run's gorge. A pleasant meadow soon comes into view to your right.

Further ahead there is a blue-blazed side trail to your left, leading to a vista cut into the forest and a register. You are given another view of Rock Run's curving gorge and the steep glen carved by Hound Run. Back on the OLP, follow another old forest grade around the edge of the plateau, with more broken vistas. The trail is mostly level as it crosses a pipeline swath, with a view to the north. It passes another register and returns you to your car.

44. **Miners Run and Band Rock Vista**

Duration: 4 hours

Distance: 6 miles

Difficulty: Very difficult—steep, rocky, rugged terrain; several stream crossings; trail is poorly blazed and not established for much of its length; off-trail hiking and bushwhacking required

Highlights: Numerous waterfalls and cascades, massive boulders, vista, charcoal mound

Elevation change: 800 feet

Directions: From Williamsport, take US 15 north toward Mansfield. At Trout Run, follow PA 14 for about 11 miles to the small village of Ralston. Upon entering Ralston, turn right after the Methodist church (which is on your left) onto Thompson Street. The street turns left, then right where it crosses over Lycoming Creek. You are now on Rock Run Road. Follow Rock Run Road for about 2.2 miles until it crosses Miners Run.

Miners Run has carved a glen of rugged and fantastic beauty into the plateau of the McIntyre Wild Area. From Rock Run Road, notice the small waterfalls both above and beneath the bridge. This is only a taste of what is to come. Pass the trail sign and follow the trail as it ascends along the right side of the stream. Here the trail is unblazed but well established. Across the stream, there is a large boulder standing on its end above a waterfall.

Follow the trail as it continues upstream. After a short distance, you have no choice but to cross the stream, as large cliffs dominate the glen. Here you will notice lime green blazes, which appear to be blazed one-way and are infrequent. Be careful as the trail makes a steep, rocky ascent beneath a rock face. The trail passes a second waterfall, several flumes, and massive boulders, where the trail crosses the stream again. Miners Run makes a tight turn around another waterfall. The terrain is very rugged, and the trail is difficult as it is traverses a steep bank. You then pass by a "boulder arch," where one end of a large boulder rests on the stream bank and the other end sits on a rounded, smaller boulder in the streambed. Miners Run flows underneath this unique arch. Be advised that the blazes in this section are infrequent as you pass more cascades and boulders.

Continue to follow Miners Run upstream as you pass another flume, more boulders, and the two largest waterfalls, with a combined height of about 50 to 60 feet. You will notice blazes on the left side of the run. Scramble to the top of the falls, and the trail crosses the run beneath a smaller waterfall and meets an established trail, an old grade. Turn left on this grade and continue upstream. On your return, you will proceed straight on this old grade heading downstream along the edge of the glen.

After a short distance, you pass an **X** painted on a tree, but the trail continues and crosses the stream to your left. Use care as you traverse another steep, rocky bank over a streambed littered with boulders and marked by small waterfalls. Cross the stream before another cliff. You cross the stream again underneath a pile of boulders laced with waterfalls and cascades. From this point to McIntyre Road, which is only a short distance ahead, there are no blazes or trail; you have to follow Miners Run upstream. Along the way, you pass one last, small waterfall and finally reach the road, which suddenly appears to your left.

To reach Band Rock Vista, turn right and hike up the road. Off to your left on the slope is a huge charcoal pile, a remnant of logging days. McIntyre Road gently ascends the plateau and passes several gated roads. The road passes a sign for the McIntyre Wild Area near a parking area sheltered by pine trees. Near here is the abandoned mining town of McIntyre. This once-vibrant town is long gone, with only sunken foundations and a cemetery remaining. The road becomes more narrow, begins a slow descent, bears left, and passes an old quarry and small stream. About .75 mile farther, the road ends, and an unblazed trail takes you to Band Rock Vista. This vista provides you with a great view of the narrow Lycoming Creek valley, Ralston, and the sloping flank of Sullivan Mountain to the south. Bodine Mountain rises even farther to the south. This vista was once known as Bandstand Rock because residents of McIntyre built a wooden platform on the rock. Each Sunday for about 15 years, a small band would play here, and it is said that residents of the valley below heard and enjoyed the music. North of here are Abbot and Dutchman Runs; both have several waterfalls but lack a trail system. Along the edge of the plateau north of Abbot Run is a spectacular series of cliffs.

To return, walk back to Miners Run and make the difficult descent to the grade mentioned previously. The grade follows the rim of the glen and offers a view of several waterfalls. Be careful, as the drop to Miners Run can be precipitous. The blazes are infrequent, but the grade continues to descend along the edge of the glen. The trail tunnels through

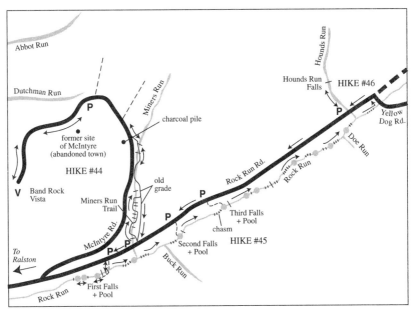

Hike 44: Miners Run and Band Rock Vista
Hike 45: Rock Run
Hike 46: Hounds Run

thick undergrowth (don't be tempted to make the steep descent back to the run), turns right, and quickly returns you to your car. The blazes become nonexistent, but if you simply follow the edge of the glen down, you will not get lost; a faint trail may provide some guidance. You return through the underbrush to the left of the trail sign.

45. Rock Run

Duration:	5 to 7 hours
Distance:	5.3 miles
Difficulty:	Very difficult—no trail; must bushwhack and follow the stream; terrain is wet, rocky, slippery, and rugged; countless stream crossings
Highlights:	Waterfalls, cliffs, erosional features, chutes, flumes, potholes, spectacular pools, cascades
Elevation change:	400 feet

Directions: From Williamsport, take US 15 north toward Mansfield. At Trout Run, follow PA 14 for about 11 miles to the small village of Ralston. Upon entering Ralston, turn right after the Methodist church (which is on your left) onto Thompson Street. The street turns left, then right where it crosses over Lycoming Creek. You are now on Rock Run Road. Follow the road for about 2 miles, until you reach a small parking area on the left. There is no sign. A trail descends from the other side of the road to Rock Run, above First Falls and Pool.

Rock Run is a hidden wonderland containing exceptional natural beauty. I first learned of Rock Run when I read several different publications that referred to it as "the most beautiful stream in Pennsylvania." Despite the fact that Pennsylvania is laced with many beautiful streams, this claim is probably true. Pennsylvania has many streams named Rock Run, but none is quite as beautiful as this one in the northeast corner of Lycoming County. This Rock Run is unique, in that its gorge and watershed are almost completely forested and untouched. Its water runs cold and clear all year long, and it is a good trout stream. Rock Run's numerous pools hold brook and brown trout. But what is most impressive about Rock Run is what it has done to the land. Most streams babble over cobblestone bottoms. Rock Run, however, has carved itself into solid rock in numerous places. There are chasms, overhanging ledges, flumes, chutes, deep pools, waterfalls, potholes, tubs, and channels carved into sandstone.

Exploring Rock Run is not a hike; it's an expedition. There are no trails following the run, and there are no blazes. Rock Run Road follows the run, but it is high on the bank and always out of sight. To explore Rock Run's beauty, you must simply walk up the run—or down it. As a result, there are numerous stream crossings. You must feel comfortable boulder-hopping, scrambling, and traversing ledges. You often have to walk in the water. You should be physically fit and take every safety precaution. All this effort will result in an experience of great beauty.

Do not even think about exploring Rock Run in high water; it is a very powerful stream, and crossing it would be dangerous. The same goes for periods of snow or ice. During high water, Rock Run becomes a ferocious white-water river with class V rapids. I once met a man who had descended Rock Run in a kayak; this radical form of kayaking is known as "steep creeking." I suggest that you explore Rock Run in summer.

Wear sandals, water shoes, or sneakers with good traction; this environment is not made for hiking boots, as your feet will get wet. Hiking poles are also a necessity to measure the depth of pools and to test the slipperiness of rocks. You may also want to bring a bathing suit, because there are some awesome pools carved into solid rock. But be advised that when I visited in August after a week of 100-degree temperatures, the water was still frigid. As I shivered next to the pool, an elderly man—a longtime resident of Ralston—reported that it was the warmest he had ever seen it; he said that the water temperature rarely rises above 60 degrees F. As I said, this is no average stream.

To begin, cross Rock Run Road from where you parked, descending along an unblazed trail as it bears to the right. Along the way, it passes the foundation and steps of an old cottage. You soon reach Rock Run, where it has carved long, deep channels into solid slabs of sandstone. It is best that you cross the run here, as there is a short trail on the other side. The run tumbles over a cascade and flume and enters a small pool. After encircling boulders and cobblestones, Rock Run tumbles over First Falls and into First Pool—a spectacular place. The pool is encircled with overhanging ledges, where you can look out over the pool and waterfall. First Falls is about 12 feet high, and its pool is large but mostly shallow, with the exception of two deep holes carved into the bedrock. The holes drop suddenly. The hole closest to the falls is about 18 feet deep with an aquamarine hue. If you are daring, it's possible to jump into this pool from the overhanging ledge. The second pool farther downstream is about 6 feet deep and is slowly filling with sediment. It appears that these holes used to be the plunge pools of ancient waterfalls.

Follow the trail a short distance downstream to where it scrambles down the ledges; this gives you an opportunity to explore the pool from below. Heading downstream, you pass a cascade, more boulders, and cobblestones. The gorge begins to narrow, with cliffs and ledges on both sides. The run passes through a flume and against several large boulders. Scramble onto a ledge to the right, where the stream enters several flumes, chutes, and more channels. You then reach a beautiful circular pool about 8 to 10 feet deep. Although people often visit the three main pools and waterfalls, you often have out-of-the-way pools, such as this one, all to yourself. Farther downstream, Rock Run tumbles over cobblestones and enters an oval pool encased with overhanging ledges. From here, backtrack to First Falls and Pool.

You head upstream for the remainder of your exploration of Rock Run until you reach Yellow Dog Road, roughly 3 miles ahead. It is generally easier to head up the run along the left bank (going upstream, not down), because it receives the greatest exposure to the sun and is less slippery. You have little choice but to traverse the left bank when hiking around Second Falls and Pool and Third Falls and Pool, because the terrain is too steep on the right bank.

Proceeding from First Falls, you pass the trail by which you arrived to your left. The run is dominated by cobblestones, small boulders, flumes, and a shallow pool. After about .25 mile, you reach an oval pool braced with ledges. Miners Run tumbles from the left. A flume and cascade caps this scenic pool. You pass two more smaller pools separated by flumes, chutes, and channels carved into solid rock. Rock Run bears to the right and rapidly descends through a huge flume clogged with boulders and framed by large, slippery ledges. Buck Run cascades beautifully from the right. Above Buck Run, there is another large, powerful flume. As you near Second Falls and Pool, the run widens over cobblestones and bears to the left.

Second Falls is probably the most visited place along Rock Run because it is the most accessible and receives the greatest exposure to the sun. Here, Rock Run has carved a narrow chasm through a massive white sandstone ledge, and it cascades into an exquisite pool about 17 feet deep. A small, deep, churning pool is within this chasm. The pool's solid rock bottom is visible through the crystal-clear water; it almost looks like a bathtub or swimming pool. As the pool heads downstream, it becomes more shallow, with a cobblestone and gravel bottom. There are some carvings in the ledges—one dating to 1938. A trail ascends to the left and joins Rock Run Road.

Above Second Falls, Rock Run bears right and becomes surrounded by large, overhanging ledges. The streambed contains large boulders, cobblestones, and several small flumes. A small seasonal stream cascades from the right. The run flows over a rock bottom, over numerous flumes, and around a smooth gray boulder. To the left are numerous ledges beneath large cliffs. Rock Run becomes more constricted within a channel, and you enter one of the most scenic sections, where the run flows through a chasm surrounded by large overhanging ledges and cliffs. You have to scramble and climb the ledges to the left. Rock Run spirals down a powerful chute and into a deep pool below. Many springs softly cascade from the right bank. The terrain through this section is particularly rugged, so use caution. The beauty is also incredible. Upon reaching the top of the ledge, head upstream to spectacular Third Falls and Pool, which is the deepest pool at 22 feet. This pool is surrounded on both banks by large overhanging ledges; its water has an emerald hue and is very cold. Swimmers often jump from both banks and return by climbing along Third Falls. This section of Rock Run is utterly beautiful. A trail to your left climbs up to Rock Run Road.

Above Third Falls, Rock Run flows over cobblestones and bears right. The run flows through more narrow channels of smooth rock, potholes, and small, deep pools. Ledges dominate the left bank. Follow the stream as it bears left against more ledges, past more pools, channels, and flumes. The streambed is primarily cobblestones above. Ledges reappear to the left, as well as a cascade and boulder. You pass a long oval pool, and cliffs rise from the left bank. Rock Run roars through a cascade into a pool and flume with several boulders. You bear right along the stream across cobblestones and gravel into a deepening pool. Scramble onto the left bank above more channels, cobblestones, and a cliff rising from the right bank. Rock Run announces its presence upstream with a flume choked with boulders and a small waterfall tumbling into a whirlpool. Large ledges make up the left bank, with a round conglomerate boulder. Above are more overhanging cliffs, which continue upstream.

Above this small waterfall, the run flows over a streambed of solid rock and around boulders and another cascade. A large cliff rises to the left, from which several springs emerge into a pool. Above, flumes and channels of smooth rock alternate with cobblestones and several deep pools. To the right, Doe Run cascades into Rock Run below more pools, beautiful flumes, and boulders. You soon reach one of the most scenic pools along Rock Run. This deep pool is completely surrounded by low, overhanging ledges beneath the forest canopy and is fed by a small waterfall. It is slippery climbing up the waterfall, so it may be better to scramble up the ledges. Above this pool is a cottage. Continuing upstream, there is a solid bed of rock with flumes, channels, and potholes and another cottage to the left. Hounds Run also joins Rock Run from the left. A unique circular chute lies ahead where the run flows equally around a boulder or exposed ledge, creating an almost perfect circle of cascading water.

As you near the bridge for Yellow Dog Road, the beauty of Rock Run continues with cascading flumes, channels, and ledges of eroded rock beneath hemlocks. Scramble up to the road, and follow it to the left, where it becomes Rock Run Road. If you didn't bring two cars, the walk back to the small parking area above First Falls and Pool is easy. Along the way, you pass small parking areas to the right. Trails descend from the road to each of the three major pools, so you can easily visit these beautiful places again, if you wish.

🚶🚶 46. Hounds Run

Duration: 1 to 2 hours

Distance: 1 mile

Difficulty: Moderate to difficult—no trail; you must bushwhack and follow the stream; very rocky, wet, and slippery, with several stream crossings

Highlights: Waterfall, cascades, isolated gorge

Elevation change: 300 feet

Directions: From Williamsport, take US 15 north toward Mansfield. At Trout Run, follow PA 14 for about 11 miles to the small village of Ralston. Upon entering Ralston, turn right after the Methodist church (which is on your left) onto Thompson Street. The street turns left, then right where it crosses over Lycoming Creek. You are now on Rock Run Road. Follow the road for about 4 miles until it crosses Hounds Run; there is a small trail sign. Park on the left side of the road.

The only thing that indicates the existence of Hounds Run Trail is the trail sign along Rock Run Road. Do not expect any blazes or an established trail. What makes this a worthwhile hike is a sizable waterfall located no more than .5 mile upstream. Because the terrain is rugged, rocky, and slippery, you will find it challenging—even frustrating.

I began by hiking up the right side of the stream. As the bank on the right side of the stream becomes steeper, you have to cross the stream and meet the remnants of an old forest road. Here, the stream has carved a steep glen. To your right is an overhanging ledge. Above this ledge, the run is carving itself into the bedrock amid cobblestones. Traversing the bottom of this glen can be difficult, as it is very rocky. Continuing upstream, there is a wide ledge with a 5-foot waterfall. This ledge is very slippery and can be difficult to cross.

Hike up the left side of the stream, where you soon see Hounds Run Falls, totaling 30 to 40 feet. The water drops over a rock face, then slides down a flume among boulders. To the right is a cliff. It's possible to reach the top of the falls by climbing a fern-covered grade off to your left. Once you reach the top, a ledge hangs over the falls and offers a nice view down the glen. This locale is rugged, with boulders, ledges, and cliffs. From here, return the way you came.

🏃🏃 47. Yellow Dog Run and Rock Run

Duration: 2 hours

Distance: 3 miles

Difficulty: Moderate—long, gradual descent and ascent; eroded and wet in spots

Highlights: Waterfall and cascades, chutes, pools, erosional features along Rock Run

Elevation change: 550 feet

Directions: From Williamsport, take US 15 north toward Mansfield. At Trout Run, follow PA 14 for about 11 miles to the small village of Ralston. Upon entering Ralston, turn right after the Methodist church (which is on your left) onto Thompson Street. The street turns left, then right where it crosses over Lycoming Creek. You are now on Rock Run Road. Follow this road in its entirety; along the way, you pass the trailheads for Hike Nos. 44, 45, and 46. After almost 4.5 miles, the road turns right, crosses Rock Run, and becomes Yellow Dog Road. Follow Yellow Dog Road as it ascends the plateau for about 2 miles. As you reach the top of the plateau, you will see the orange blazes of the Old Loggers Path (OLP) where the road makes a sharp left turn. There are a few spaces to park along the left side of the road.

This short, scenic hike utilizes the orange-blazed OLP and explores one of its most scenic sections. Because it is not a loop, you will have to return the way you came. From the small parking area, follow the OLP up Yellow Dog Road. After a short distance, turn left into the forest and make a slight descent from the road. The trail crosses the headwaters of Yellow Dog Run and meets an old forest road, where it turns left. The trail passes by a small stream and several springs, making portions of this trail wet and eroded. You begin descending into Yellow Dog Run's small glen. Unfortunately, like most trails, this one is high above the run. The forest along the trail is dominated by hardwoods, with scattered hemlocks, and it appears to be healthy, unlike many forests on top of the plateau.

The trail continues its descent. Be careful, as the trail can be rocky and eroded where small streams have eaten away at the old forest road. After about .75 mile, you should hear a waterfall deep in the glen. This gentle waterfall is about 20 feet high and can be seen from the trail

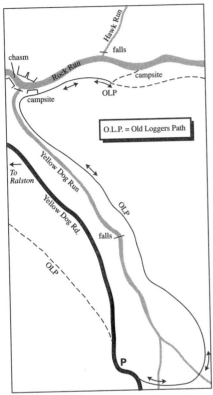

Hike 47: Yellow Dog Run and Rock Run

when the trees are bare. There is no side trail to this pretty waterfall. Follow the trail as it makes its descent all the way to Rock Run.

You soon reach the highlight of this hike—the juncture of Yellow Dog and Rock Runs. Here, Yellow Dog Run sweeps over a rock face into a small chasm created by Rock Run. Rock Run is an exceptionally beautiful stream. Here, it has carved itself into the bedrock, creating chasms, chutes, and deep pools. The water is crystal clear and cold. You will probably want to spend some time here. If you want to explore more of Rock Run downstream, see Hike No. 45.

The trail turns right and follows Rock Run upstream. At places, the run is out of sight, but it is not far away and can be easily reached. Notice the overhanging ledges, boulders, and pools within the run. Keep an eye out where Hawk Run makes a small waterfall into Rock Run on the other bank. If you want to wade or swim, be prepared for cold water, even in the summer. Rock Run is by far the coldest freestone stream I've encountered—even colder than some limestone streams.

Continue to follow the trail upstream until you reach the point where the trail begins to make a steep ascent away from the run and passes a campsite. It is about .3 mile from Yellow Dog Run. From here, return the way you came.

48. Sand Spring Trail (Devil's Elbow Natural Area)

Duration:	2 hours
Distance:	3 miles
Difficulty:	Easy—mostly flat; rocky and wet in sections
Highlights:	Hemlocks, several swamps and bogs
Elevation change:	100 feet

Directions: From Forksville, follow PA 154 to Shunk. At Shunk, avoid PA 154, which makes a sharp right. Continue straight on SR 4002 to the tiny village of Tomkins Corners. Continue straight to Ellenton, where you follow the road when it makes a sharp right. From Ellenton, the road (SR 1013) eventually enters Tiadaghton State Forest. After driving about 3.5 miles from Ellenton, you will notice a parking area on the left, a sign for Hawkeye Cross Country Ski Trails, and the Sand Spring Trail in Devil's Elbow Natural Area.

This hike explores a scenic hardwood forest and wraps around emergent shrub and forested wetlands. The trail uses old forest roads and grades and crosses several streams and springs. Due to the high elevation—between 2,200 and 2,300 feet—the natural area is home to unique flora and wildlife. Numerous orchids and pitcher plants can be found here in summer. Parts of this trail are ideal for cross-country skiing. The trail is blazed powder blue. Unlike some plateau forests, which have suffered from insect infestation, the hardwood forest here is mostly healthy.

From the parking area across the road, you pass a trail sign and a gate. The trail begins as a grassy forest road. After a short distance, you pass two old forest roads to the left; the second is your return route. Continue straight along an electric deer fence. After about .5 mile, the trail begins to narrow as ferns encroach, and it continues a gentle ascent.

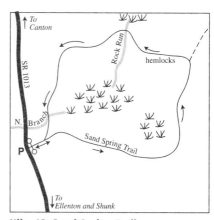

Hike 48: Sand Spring Trail

Follow the trail as it veers left under hemlocks and makes a gradual descent. The forest here is particularly scenic, with stately hardwoods and deep green hemlocks. Watch for blazes where the trail makes a sharp left. This place can be tricky, because another obvious trail continues straight. At this point, the trail no longer follows an old forest road as it tunnels under hemlock saplings. The terrain is rocky, and the trail is often wet. Hemlocks dominate this section, giving it a deep, dark feel. The trail passes a spring and crosses a small creek. There is a swamp only a short distance upstream. This creek is the source of the North Branch of Rock Run.

The trail continues straight, following the remnants of another old forest road. It bears left and descends to the edge of a large scenic wetland with silvery snags. Wildlife abounds in this wetland. Cross the stream as best you can. The trail follows the edge of the stream for a short distance before it bears left and makes a gradual ascent to complete the loop; turn right to return to your car.

Tioga County and State Forest (Eastern Section)

Tioga State Forest is best known for the spectacular Pine Creek Gorge. However, there are scenic areas in its eastern section that are worthy of exploration. This section is dominated by isolated plateaus, with views and waterfalls. Here, the snow often lingers into April, offering great opportunities for snowmobiling or cross-country skiing. These plateaus also contain coal, and irresponsible mining has caused some streams, such as Fall Brook, to become polluted. This was one of the first areas in Pennsylvania where coal was mined and produced. In the 1800s, when coal was king, Fall Brook was home to more than 2,000 people. After being ravaged by smallpox and threatened by forest fires, the town declined. Now there is nothing there to speak of, with the exception of a few hunting cabins.

Contact information: Tioga State Forest, One Nessmuk Lane, Wellsboro, PA 16901; phone: 570-724-2868; website: www.dcnr.state.pa.us/forestry; e-mail: fd16@state.pa.us

🏃🏃 49. Fall Brook Falls

Duration:	½ hour

Distance:	.25 mile

Difficulty: Easy—use caution hiking along the edge of the glen or descending into it

Highlights: Waterfalls

Elevation change: 100 feet

Directions: Proceed north from Williamsport along US 15. Exit the highway at Trout Run and proceed north along PA 14 until about 3 miles before Canton, where you make a left onto PA 414. Follow PA 414 for about 3 miles until you reach the tiny village of Gleason. Here, PA 414 makes a sharp left turn, and another paved road joins from the right, making a T; turn right onto this road. You should see a sign for the County Bridge Picnic Area. After a few miles, this road becomes a wide dirt road. Follow this road for about 5 miles until you reach the picnic area. At the picnic area is another T; turn left. Follow this dirt road up and over the plateau, through scenic plantations of pine trees, and down the other side for almost 3 miles. Once you descend from the plateau, you pass a road on the right and a small bridge over a stream. This is Fall Brook. There is a parking area on the left; there is no sign.

Because it is so short, a visit to Fall Brook Falls isn't much of a hike. But it is such a scenic and isolated place that it is worthy of your attention. Fall Brook Falls used to be a popular picnic area. Fortunately for you, the people have gone with the picnic tables, and it appears to be forgotten. This trail is unblazed.

From the small parking area, go around the gate and follow the grassy forest road a short distance until the trail makes a left and crosses a small stone bridge into a beautiful grove of pine and hemlock trees. To your left is Fall Brook, stained orange from acid mine drainage. There isn't an established trail through this grove, so stay close to the stream, which is to your left. The trail descends along Fall Brook and comes to the first waterfall, about 15 or 20 feet high. There is a galvanized pipe railing along the trail above the waterfalls. Fall Brook has carved a scenic rocky glen, with cliffs and overhanging ledges. In fact, it's hard to get a good look at some of the waterfalls because the ledges

almost hang over them. Immediately below the first waterfall is
another about the same height,
along with several more cascades
and small waterfalls that descend
over the ledges and large boulders
strewn in the streambed. At the
end of the railing, heading downstream, it is possible to climb down
into the glen between the cliffs, but
use caution as you descend. The
view looking up to the waterfalls is
well worth the effort.

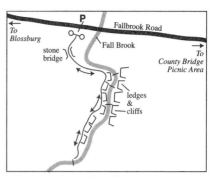

Hike 49: Fall Brook Falls

If you look carefully, there is a narrow trail that traverses the edge of
the glen downstream, overlooking the last series of cascades. Be careful hiking this section, as it is rocky and follows the edge of the ledges.
This trail makes a steep descent to a last cascade and pool. Here, Fall
Brook leaves its rocky glen and continues on to the Tioga River. Return
the way you came.

50. Sand Run Falls

Duration: 3 to 4 hours

Distance: 7 miles

Difficulty: Moderate—mild inclines and declines; rocky, wet, and entangled
with roots in spots

Highlights: Scenic glen with waterfall, seasonal waterfalls

Elevation change: 400 feet

Directions: Proceeding north on US 15 from the Williamsport area, exit at
Blossburg. Bear right onto SR 2017. Just south of Blossburg, turn right onto
SR 2016 and pass under the US 15 bridge. Drive through the small village
of Arnot, and follow the road as it turns right. Turn left onto a dirt road
about 2.5 miles from Arnot. There is a sign there for Sand Run Trail. The
parking area is a short distance up this road. If you cross the bridge over
Sand Run, you went too far.

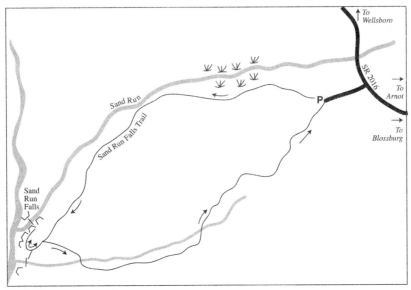

Hike 50: Sand Run Falls

This scenic loop, blazed orange, features Sand Run Falls near the confluence of Sand Run and Babb Creek. This trail was initially established by Daren Bryant for his Eagle Scout project and is currently maintained by Troop 24 in Wellsboro. From the small parking area, begin the loop from the north side of the road, passing the trail sign with a map etched in wood. The forest here is typical of the high plateau—an open hardwood forest with an occasional understory of brush and saplings. Hemlocks dominate the gentle glen carved by Sand Run. This trail is unusual, in that you have to hike downstream to see a waterfall.

You pass a register and, soon thereafter, a spring. Wetlands, through which Sand Run meanders, lie to your right. At first, Sand Run is out of sight, but it eventually comes into view. You pick up an old grade or forest road and pass a beaver dam in the run. The trail makes a slight descent, and a blue-blazed ski trail joins from the left. Traverse the edge of a bank above the run between hemlocks to your right and hardwoods to your left. The trail descends through hemlock saplings and bears left on another grade. You traverse the edge of Sand Run's deep glen and begin to descend.

The trail soon reaches the end of the loop. Bear left on the spur trail to see Sand Run Falls. In times of sufficient rain, you may hear a small stream off to your left. Where the trail makes a sharp right, notice an obvious, unblazed path to the left. After a very short distance, this path reaches a small stream above a 15-foot waterfall.

Back on the trail, continue to follow the spur to reach Sand Run Falls. The waterfall is surrounded by fractured cliffs and ledges and tumbles into a plunge pool. Although the trail brochure states that the falls is 30 feet high, this may be an overestimate. Campsites lie beneath the falls, near where Sand Run joins Babb Creek. This spot is very scenic.

Return to the loop, and begin your return hike. The trail makes a gradual ascent. Pay attention where the trail makes a sharp right and crosses the small stream mentioned previously. You immediately turn left on another old grade. Heading upstream, the trail passes large boulders and ledges and crosses the stream again. You pass around the edge of an open, grassy area, and the trail picks up an old forest road. The forest along this return hike is very open, and some logging has taken place. The blue-blazed ski trail again joins from the left. Make a left onto a grassy road, from which you turn left again. The trail passes another register and soon returns you to your car.

🚶🚶 51. C. Lynn Keller Trail

Duration:	3 to 4 hours
Distance:	5.6 miles
Difficulty:	Moderate—long ascent and descent; a few steep, rocky sections
Highlights:	Scenic woodlands, mountain laurel, partial view
Elevation change:	1,100 feet

Directions: From Mansfield, proceed north on US 15. As you near the exit, you'll be driving above Tioga Lake. Exit at PA 287, and turn left to the town of Tioga. Pay attention where PA 287 makes a sharp right in the middle of Tioga. PA 287 passes along the shore of Hammond Lake. Make a left to the Ives Run Boat Launch and Recreation Area. Cross over a bridge, and pass the boat launch and picnic area to your left. Turn right onto a state game land dirt road. Parking for the trailhead is immediately on your right. Most of this trail is located on State Game Lands (SGL) 37.

Contact information: Pennsylvania Game Commission, Northcentral Regional Office, PO Box 5038, Jersey Shore, PA 17740; phone: 570-398-4744 or 877-877-7674; website: www.pgc.state.pa.us. Also, Tioga-Hammond/Cowanesque Lakes, RD #1, Box 65, Tioga, PA 16946-9733; phone: 570-835-5281.

The C. Lynn Keller Trail is located in SGL 37 and the Ives Run Recreation Area located along Hammond Lake. The trail was named after a Pennsylvania district game protector who died of leukemia in 1978. From the small parking area on Stephenhouse Road, the trail begins at a sign and map located along the road. This section of the hike is blazed a yellowish cream color. The trail begins a gradual ascent that becomes increasingly steeper. The forest is dominated by open hardwoods with pine, hemlock, witch hazel, and mountain laurel. After the steep ascent, the trail levels and passes flaking boulders of sandstone. You soon cross a grassy swath, and the trail follows an old forest road. Hike up the mild ascent to reach a trail sign. You will return to this point after completing the loop you're about to hike.

Turn right onto a red-blazed trail that crosses patches of laurel. The trail is initially level but begins a gradual ascent along a small seasonal stream to your left. As you ascend the glen, the trail becomes increasingly steep, and you pass paper birch trees on your left. Bear right as the trail levels off and reaches the top of the ridge. Just ahead is another trail sign. A short spur takes you to an overgrown vista offering partial views in the winter from an exposed ledge. At the sign, turn left and follow the trail, now blazed yellow. The hard part is mostly over. The trail is level, with gradual ascents as it traverses the ridge. When you reach an unblazed, grassy forest road, fol-

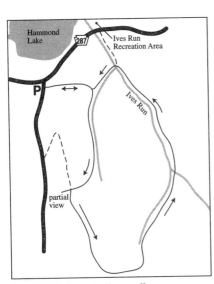

Hike 51: C. Lynn Keller Trail

low it for a short distance, and turn left where the trail reenters the forest. The trail is again blazed yellow.

You now begin a long descent along another old forest road, passing through thick stands of laurel and crossing rivulets. The trail eventually crosses a small stream and passes through an abandoned field overgrown with brush. At trail sign, turn left and pass through an abandoned orchard. Upon reaching another trail sign, turn left to hike the remaining .4 mile back to complete the loop. The trail to the right passes through brush and ends near the campsites, pavilions, and playing fields of the Ives Run Recreation Area. Once you complete the loop (at the first trail sign you reached), turn right to complete the return hike.

Bradford County

In both population and land area, Bradford County is the largest in the Endless Mountains. The western and southern sections are dominated by plateaus, and the remainder comprises rolling farms and isolated mountains. The Susquehanna River, with its wide valley, flows down the center of the county, often underneath towering cliffs. Bradford County is also home to several scenic towns, such as Troy and Towanda. This rural county is unusual, in that it has a fine system of municipal and county parks.

Bradford County's historic claim to fame is the French Azilum, located between Wysox and Wyalusing. It is believed that Queen Marie Antoinette hoped to find refuge here during the French Revolution. Unfortunately, she never had the chance to witness the beauty that awaited her.

🚶🚶 52. Lambs Vista

Duration: ¹/₂ hour

Distance: .25 mile

Difficulty: Easy—you can drive to the vista

Highlights: Beautiful vista

Elevation change: Minimal

Directions: From the stoplight in Canton, proceed north on PA 14 toward Troy. About .5 mile from the stoplight, turn left onto Upper Mountain Road. This road eventually becomes a dirt road and begins to climb up the mountain. As you near the top, make the first right on Lambs Park Road and pass a house on your left. After about .25 mile, make the first left on another dirt road, which wraps around and makes a gradual climb to the vista.

Contact information: Tioga State Forest, One Nessmuk Lane, Wellsboro, PA 16901; phone: 570-724-2868; website: www.dcnr.state.pa.us/forestry; e-mail: fd16@state.pa.us

Because you can drive to Lambs Vista, it is definitely not a hike. Regardless, I included it in this guide because it is relatively unknown and offers a tremendous vista to the east—a rarity in the Endless Mountains. The vista's elevation is approximately 2,300 feet, some 1,000 feet above the surrounding farmlands.

Lambs Vista overlooks the dairy farms of Bradford County. In summer, these farmlands look like a patchwork quilt of tan, brown, and green, and their silos shine in the sunlight. To the southwest rises the sharp escarpment of Leroy and Barclay Mountains. These mountains are part of the Glaciated High Plateau and hold Sunfish Pond (Hike No. 53) and the watershed of beautiful Schrader Creek. Sunrises are said to be memorable from this vista. On the clearest days, you may even be able to see East and Elk Mountains in eastern Susquehanna County.

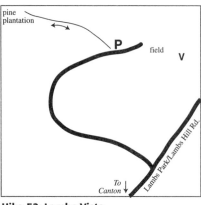

Hike 52: Lambs Vista

An old forest road behind the picnic area passes through a hardwood forest and diminishes at a large pine plantation. This vista offers no other trails, but it is a great place to picnic, relax, or just enjoy the view.

53. Sunfish Pond County Park

Duration:	Less than 1 hour
Distance:	1 mile
Difficulty:	Easy—level, but rocky and wet in parts
Highlights:	Scenic, isolated mountaintop lake
Elevation change:	30 feet

Directions: From US 220 at Monroeton, south of Towanda, take PA 414 west toward Canton. After about 13 miles, you reach the tiny village of Le Roy. Turn left onto Leroy Mountain Road (SR 3010); there should be a small green sign indicating Sunfish Pond County Park. Follow this road straight through an intersection. You begin to make a steep climb up the mountain, turning left where the road passes a small stream with several cascades. Upon reaching a T at the top of the plateau, turn right, following the road as it winds through a scenic grove of spruce and pine. Upon entering the park, the road turns left. The Up Top Stop is on your left.

Contact information: Phone: 570-265-1727; websites: www.bradford-pa.com and www.endlessmountains.org

Sunfish Pond is a beautiful place to visit and offers a short, scenic hike. The park is surrounded by State Game Lands 12 and is one of the most isolated places in the Endless Mountains. Sunfish Pond is a fine place to go fishing or just explore by canoe or kayak. The pond is located near the top of the plateau, at over 2,000 feet elevation, and is surrounded by thousands of acres of forest. Campsites are available along the northern and eastern shores of the pond.

One of the greatest aspects of Sunfish Pond is its isolation. There is no noise from towns or highways. Everything is still and serene. If you camp overnight, expect an amazing showcase of stars.

From the small parking area at the Up Top Stop, bear left (south), and walk down the paved road. The road passes mountain laurel, hemlock, and pine. To your right is Sunfish Pond. As you continue

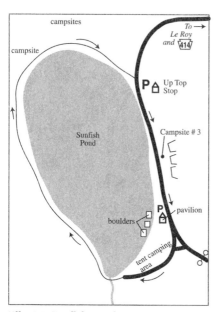

Hike 53: Sunfish Pond County Park

hiking, 20-foot sandstone ledges rise behind Campsite #3, to your left. You pass a small parking area and a pavilion. The southern shore is dotted with white boulders, and the bottom of the pond appears to be rocky, making it likely that Sunfish Pond was the work of glaciers. Much of the shoreline is ringed with small white boulders of sandstone and conglomerate.

Turn right onto a dirt road that accesses primitive campsites. The dirt road ends at a small parking area, and the trail crosses the pond's outlet. The trail bears right as it traverses the western shore. Although unblazed, the trail is clearly established. You hike through an open hardwood forest, and brush and laurel hide the pond from view. As you near the northern end, the brush diminishes, and there are views across Sunfish Pond. Upon reaching the trail's end, turn right behind a campsite and cross a small stream. Return to your car by walking along the grassy shore to the paved road and the Up Top Stop.

54. Falls Creek

Duration:	4 to 5 hours

Distance:	2 miles

Difficulty: Very difficult. There is no trail ascending Falls Creek. You must scramble, bushwhack, rock-hop, and cross the stream several times. The terrain is very rocky and rugged. Bypassing Bradford Falls is the most difficult part, as it is very steep, with loose footing. Do not attempt during periods of high water or ice.

Highlights: Spectacular waterfalls and cascades; scenic, isolated glen, cliffs, boulders, ledges

Elevation change: 650 feet

Directions: From US 220 at Monroeton, take PA 414 west toward Canton. After about 2.6 miles, you reach the small village of Powell, where you make a sharp left onto Main Street (a school is ahead on the right). You cross over Towanda Creek and then Schrader Creek. After crossing Schrader Creek, make a right onto Weston Road. After driving almost 2 miles, you come to a Y, where you bear right; Falls Creek is about 6.1 miles farther. You cross Schrader Creek again and enter its scenic gorge. After 3 miles, you pass an impressive series of ledge-formed rapids to your left. The road climbs high above Schrader Creek and makes a gradual descent before crossing Falls Creek over a small, narrow concrete bridge. There is a small parking area to your right before the bridge, but no sign. If you reach a Y in the road among cottages, you went a mile too far.

To reach Barclay and its cemetery, from the trailhead, head up the road for about a mile until you come to the Y. Make a right and follow the road up along Coal Run. Near the top, avoid the road that steeply descends from the left. Instead, continue straight for a short distance, then make a very sharp left. This is where Barclay is located; the sunken foundations can still be seen. Park where you can. A short distance ahead is a four-way intersection. The road to the right eventually leads to Sunfish Pond (Hike No. 53). You will see a narrow road straight ahead, heading south. The cemetery is located down this road.

To reach the site of Laquin, head up the road from the trailhead. When you reach the Y, continue to the left. The remains of the town are roughly 3 miles from the trailhead.

Contact information: Pennsylvania Game Commission, Northeast Regional Headquarters, PO Box 220, Dallas, PA 18612-0220; phone: 570-675-1143 or 877-877-9357; website: www.pgc.state.pa.us

The history of this region is remarkable. This area is one of the most isolated in the Endless Mountains and eastern Pennsylvania. You will find extensive forests, a few open fields, meadows, and hunting cabins. It was not always this way. Numerous coal towns were located atop Barclay Mountain, and a lumber town, Laquin, was along Schrader Creek. In 1812, a hunter discovered coal on top of Barclay Mountain. By 1856, a settlement was established, and coal was commercially mined. This vibrant community was known as Barclay and had churches, schools, and even a bar. At its height, Barclay had a population of over 2,000, and its mines produced 300,000 tons of coal annually. The people of Barclay came primarily from Ireland, Wales, and Scotland; they created a close-knit community. Five satellite towns were built around Barclay: Falls Creek, Graydon, Dublin, Foot of Plane, and Carbon Run.

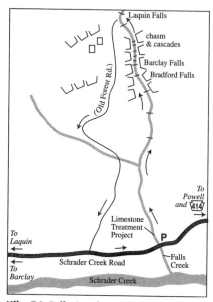

Hike 54: Falls Creek

In 1884–85, the town was struck with a diphtheria epidemic, and many children died. Today you can still visit Barclay's large, fascinating cemetery, where these children were buried. By 1900, Barclay had all but disappeared.

Another interesting regional feature was the incline plane. To transport coal from the top of the plateau to the S&NY Railroad along Schrader Creek (the remains of which can still be seen today), an incline plane was constructed with a pulley. When one car went down, it pulled another up.

With the expiration of Barclay, the focus turned from coal to lumber. Laquin was established in 1902 along Schrader Creek, and it had all the right ingredients: a railroad, water, and tens of thousands of forested acres. Lumber mills were erected that produced millions of board feet, along with kindling, barrel staves, wagon wheels, and hubs. A chemical plant and tannery were also constructed. When the lumber in the Schrader tract was depleted, lumber was imported to Laquin from tracts in Wyoming and Sullivan Counties. By 1925, there were no more tracts to exploit, and the lumber mill closed. The chemical plant closed in 1932. Ironically, it was the depression that provided Laquin's last bit of life support. A Civilian Conservation Corps camp was built in Laquin in 1933, where the workers replanted the forests that had been destroyed. With the ending of the depression and the beginning of World War II, Laquin finally met its fate in 1941. At its height, the town had over 2,000 people and about 110 buildings. Like Barclay, Laquin was a vibrant town; it even had a local baseball team. How these large towns could disappear without a trace is astonishing.

Isolated and without a trail system, Falls Creek first attracted my attention because of its name. Any creek with the name "falls" is bound to have a waterfall. Falls Creek is yet another waterfall gem in the Endless Mountains, and it appears to be nearly unknown. This rugged, scenic glen features about 10 waterfalls and large cascades ranging from 12 to almost 100 feet in height, along with countless small cascades. This is a very difficult hike, especially when you near the large waterfalls. There is no trail, so you have to follow the creek upstream to see all the waterfalls. Fortunately, an old forest road climbs along the west side of the glen and offers a convenient return.

From the parking area, you immediately notice a limestone treatment project. This project siphons the creek's water from a small dam upstream, circulates the water with limestone to control acidity, and returns the water to the streambed. Thanks to old mines at its headwaters, Falls Creek suffers from acid mine drainage. Fortunately, the problem is not as severe as in other streams in the area, and the rocks in the streambed are only slightly tinged orange.

As you hike up the glen, the creek tumbles over numerous boulder-formed cascades. Large boulders and cobblestones litter the stream. Compared with hiking up other streams in this guide, ascending Falls Creek is a little easier; it is a small stream, and the many boulders enable you to cross it. You have to cross the stream when one bank becomes too steep, but I generally hike up along the left bank. At times, there seem to be remnants of an old grade. After about .3 mile, a small tributary tumbles from the left. Bear right and follow Falls Creek. The stream's gradient steepens, and cascades become more pronounced. The first waterfall comes into view as it drops over a ledge and slides down a chute; it is about 15 feet high. Soon thereafter, the second waterfall can be seen as it drops over ledges, in between boulders, and down a chute. This scenic falls is about 30 feet high. The third waterfall is a 12-foot sheet of water dropping over a ledge into a pool. The surrounding glen contains many unique plants, including pitcher plants, painted trillium, phlox, and violets.

If you look around at this third waterfall, you will notice high cliffs and ledges of fractured sandstone encasing the glen. The top of a wide, monstrous waterfall can be seen as it drops over a spectacular, multicolored cliff. At about 100 feet, this is one of the highest and most impressive waterfalls in the Endless Mountains. This spot is utterly astonishing. To reach the bottom of this waterfall, you have to climb over logs, boulders, and cobblestones. The streambed is clogged with debris. What is most interesting is the number of decaying hemlock logs littering the streambed. They appear to be cut uniformly. During the logging era, hemlock was prized for its bark, but not its wood. Hemlock trees were cut down, stripped of their bark, and left by the loggers. These logs may have subsequently washed over the falls. I named this magnificent waterfall Bradford Falls, after the county in which it is located.

You are now faced with the most difficult and dangerous part of this hike. Because Bradford Falls is surrounded by enormous cliffs and ledges, you must backtrack and climb the right, or eastern, bank to see the many waterfalls above. Extreme care and caution are required. The bank is steep, with loose footing. If you climb the left, or western, bank, you will intersect the old forest road, your return route. I think you can get a better view of the remaining waterfalls by passing over Bradford Falls via the right bank. Once you reach the top of the bank, hike upstream along the rim of the glen. The terrain is steep and dangerous. You pass through mountain laurel and hemlock. Upon bypassing the crest of Bradford Falls, make the gradual descent back to Falls Creek. There is a limited view from the top of Bradford Falls; just don't get too close to the edge. Immediately above Bradford Falls is another waterfall. This hidden, 40-foot falls drops over a rock face. I named this waterfall Barclay Falls, after the mining town that once existed at the top of the plateau, near the source of Falls Creek.

To bypass Barclay Falls, retrace your steps up the bank, hike around it, and go back down to Falls Creek. This bypass is not nearly as difficult as the one around Bradford Falls. Continuing upstream, there is a 12-foot cascade below a staircase of small cascades. You are near the top of the plateau, and the creek flows through a tight chasm of 20-foot cliffs. Several flumes and chutes are above the cascades. As long as the water is not too high, it is possible to hike up the stream by hopping from boulder to boulder. Below a 15-foot waterfall, ascend the left bank to reach the old forest road. The final waterfall lies just upstream. I named this one Laquin Falls, after a nearby tanning and lumber town, now abandoned. It is a twin waterfall leaping over a ledge.

To return to your car, follow an old forest road. Avoid the road bearing right near the top two falls. The unblazed road descends gradually and passes large ledges and boulders to your right. At one point, you can see two large, square-shaped boulders; a faint trail to your left goes to the rim of the glen above Bradford Falls. Back on the old forest road, you continue to descend through an open hardwood forest. The trail passes more ledges and boulders to your right. The trail bears right and then turns left, meeting the small tributary described previously. You descend along this small stream until the trail turns right and crosses it. Descending along the edge of the glen, you may see glimpses of Falls Creek below. The trail gradually veers to the right, crosses several blowdowns, and reaches the road. Turn left and walk the short distance to your car.

Below the parking area, Falls Run tumbles under an old railroad bridge and joins beautiful Schrader Creek. This creek is a little smaller than the Loyalsock, but just as scenic. Some of the mountains to the north are crowned with exposed rimrock cliffs. If there were a trail to these cliffs, they would provide incredible vistas. When there is sufficient water, Schrader Creek is an excellent white-water river with class II–IV rapids. Below Falls Creek, there is a long boulder garden. Schrader Creek flows up against cliffs, across pools, and over numerous rapids. The creek is enveloped by a natural, isolated setting. About 3 miles downstream, the creek cuts through several ledges of bedrock, creating impressive rapids. These rapids can be seen from the road. If you have time, I suggest that you explore Schrader Creek along the old railroad grade (the former S&NY Railroad) that follows parts of the creek.

55. Mount Pisgah State and County Parks

Duration: 3 hours

Distance: 6 miles

Difficulty: Moderate—long ascent over a gentle trail; can be steep in sections

Highlights: Vistas

Elevation change: 1,200 feet

Directions: Mount Pisgah State Park is located about 2 miles north of US 6, about 11 miles west of Towanda. It can be reached by secondary roads; follow the park signs. If you're coming from Towanda, at the small village of West Burlington, turn right onto Wallace or Bailey's Corner Road (SR 3019). Upon reaching State Park Road, make a right and enter the park. The parking area is the fishing access area on your right, along the shore of the lake.

Contact information: Mount Pisgah State Park, RR #3, Box 362A, Troy, PA 16947-9448; phone: 570-297-2734; website: www.dcnr.state.pa.us/stateparks; e-mail: mtpisgahsp@state.pa.us. Mount Pisgah County Park, phone: 570-265-1727; websites: www.bradford-pa.com and www.endlessmountains.org.

From the parking area, follow the yellow-blazed Oh! Susanna Trail along the lake to your right. The trail crosses in between the lakeshore and State Park Road. Where the Oh! Susanna Trail makes a sharp left and crosses a stream, look across the road to your right and see a sign for Ridge Trail. This 2.4-mile trail traverses the ridge to the summit of Mount Pisgah and its numerous vistas.

The trail begins as a wide, grassy path crossing a field of goldenrod. It is mostly unblazed, but you may see occasional faded orange blazes. A snowmobile trail joins from the left, and after further ascent, another wide trail joins from the right. The trail levels off, enters the forest, and ascends through a tight S curve, passing a bench. It was here that I saw a red squirrel scamper up an oak tree. This trail is wide and well maintained all the way to the summit.

The Avery Crossover Trail leaves from the right, and you will notice an old stone wall. The trail passes many birch trees and another bench. In a classic fashion, the trail makes relatively short ascents, separated by periods of level hiking. Some of these ascents are steep, but they are generally not difficult. You climb to an area of hemlocks, after which an unmarked trail descends to the right. The trail passes along the edge of private property, and before entering a large field, Hicks Hollow Trail descends to the right. This field is a great place for wildflowers and to watch wildlife, especially wild turkey and deer. The summit of Mount Pisgah can be clearly seen off to your right.

Upon reaching the other side of the field, the trail makes a winding ascent through the forest. You pass another bench and a field off to your left. The trail levels off again and passes a gate, marking the boundary between the state and county parks. After hiking through a small glade along the edge of the mountain, the trail descends and passes another unmarked trail to your right. The trail reaches County Park Road, where you make a right. You are immediately treated to a view overlooking farmlands to the northeast.

Follow the road as it makes a gradual ascent past primitive campsites and rest rooms. Before turning left to the summit, you pass two more vistas offering views to the north and northeast. The road makes one last ascent to a microwave tower and pavilion. Here is the best vista of all—an expansive view to the west. Armenia Mountain rises prominently as you look over the town of Troy and its environs. If you have the time, I suggest that you camp on top of Mount Pisgah. It is one of the few places in Pennsylvania offering mountaintop campsites.

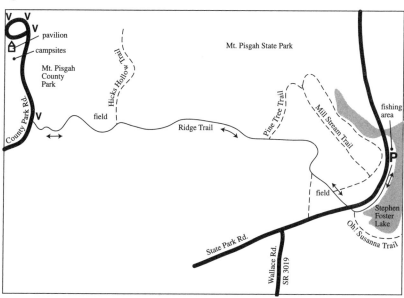

Hike 55: Mount Pisgah State and County Parks

Some of the campsites are located at the views mentioned previously. I will never forget camping here on a crisp October night, watching the sunset and the lights of Troy. But what was most spectacular was the amazing number of stars across the night sky. If you camp here, be prepared for wind. After enjoying the views, return the way you came.

Mount Pisgah State Park offers other hiking opportunities for beginners. The Oh! Susanna Trail is an easy 2.7-mile loop encircling Stephen Foster Lake. The trail passes wetlands, open fields, and scenic forests of hemlock, pine, and various hardwoods. Mill Stream Trail is blazed white and is a 1.1-mile loop. It follows the inlet to Stephen Foster Lake and its wetlands. On its return, the trail crosses the flank of the mountain, passing some boulders and ledges.

56. Round Top Park

Duration:	2 to 3 hours

Distance: 2.5 miles

Difficulty: Moderate—some steep ascents and descents; rocky and eroded in sections

Highlights: Views

Elevation change: 300 feet

Directions: From Towanda, proceed north on US 220 toward Sayre. Upon reaching the small village of Greens Landing, just south of Sayre, make the first left onto Wolcott Hollow Road (SR 4018). There should be a sign for the park. After passing a trailer court, turn right onto Murray Creek Road. Make your first right, turn right again at a T, and then bear left into the park. There are signs to direct your way. As you drive into the park, turn left just beyond the pond. The parking area is ahead, near a playing field.

Contact information: Round Top Park, phone: 570-888-2325; websites: www.bradford-pa.com and www.endlessmountains.org

Round Top Park, located in Athens Township near the New York border, is famous for its vistas. The park's trail system contains numerous connector trails, creating countless hiking options. At the parking area, you will see a sign for a model airplane flying field along a dirt road blazed red. Take this road. The road follows the edge of the mountain and offers broken views of the Chemung Valley below in winter. The road makes a gradual ascent, passing a pine plantation and a blue-blazed connector trail to your left. After making a slight turn to the left on the road, you come to an open field to your left—the model airplane flying field. To your right are blue and yellow blazes for the park's extensive mountain bike trail system. After the flying field, leave the road and turn left onto a yellow-blazed trail. This half-loop trail ascends through the forest and soon returns to the road. Bear left on the road, continuing to ascend as you pass another blue-blazed connector trail. The road bears left, passes a woods road to the right, and continues its winding ascent.

You soon reach a gate to your right; the trail makes a sharp left and begins a steep ascent. Off to your right is a parking area with a wooden sign mapping the various mountain bike and ATV trails in the park. Turn left and begin the ascent to the radio tower. Upon reaching the tower, the trail makes a steep, eroded descent with a narrow view of the mountains to the south. The trail passes both of the blue-blazed connector trails mentioned previously and arrives at a brushy meadow offering more views to the south. You soon come to a four-way intersection, and the red blazes seem to disappear. I believe that the trail to your left returns to the parking area. Continue straight on the yellow-blazed trail. It makes a gradual descent until it bears left and makes a quick climb up the embankment of a small oval pond. Hike along the pond until you reach the road. The yellow blazes follow the road to the left (the same road you used

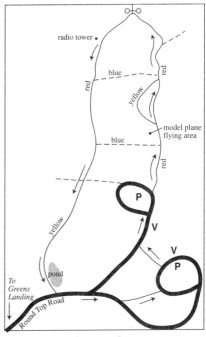

Hike 56: Round Top Park

to reach the parking area). Follow the other road off to your right and ascend a grassy power-line swath. At the top, there are playing fields, playgrounds, picnic tables, and pavilions. Turn left on the paved road. You may see signs to your right asking you not to feed the bears. I failed to see a single bear while hiking through this popular park.

Upon reaching the vista, this hike suddenly seems worthwhile. From here, the towns of South Waverly, Sayre, and Athens can be clearly seen. The Susquehanna River flows off to the east. It is difficult to see the Chemung River, which hugs the base of the mountain you are on. The hills of southern New York rise to the north.

To continue the hike, walk around the guardrail and descend the grassy swath to the left of the vista. You soon reach the paved road you used to reach the parking area. Turn right on this road. You pass a wooden sign to your left with a trail map. As you near the parking area, there is another spectacular vista to your right, looking to the east. Your car is just ahead.

Hiking Clubs and Organizations

Are you looking for friends to hike with? Do you want to help preserve and maintain Pennsylvania's hiking trails? If so, you may want to contact these regional clubs and organizations. A more complete list is on the Keystone Trail Association's website: www.kta-hike.org/clubs. Also, your local YMCA may have a hiking program. The state forests and parks are always looking for volunteers to help maintain trails.

Allentown Hiking Club
PO Box 1542
Allentown, PA 18105-1542
610-432-5652

Alpine Club of Williamsport
PO Box 501
Williamsport, PA 17701
www.angelfire.com/pa2/alpineclub
alpineclub@usa.net

Appalachian Mountain Club—Delaware Valley Chapter
1180 Greenleaf Drive
Bethlehem, PA 18017-9391
610-694-8677
www.amcdv.org

Blue Mountain Eagle Climbing Club
PO Box 14982
Reading, PA 19612
www.bmecc.org

Eagles Mere Conservancy
Eagles Mere, PA 17731-0064
570-525-3725
www.eaglesmere.org/conservancy.html

Keystone Trails Association
PO Box 129
Confluence, PA 15424-0129
www.kta-hike.org

Mid State Trail Association
PO Box 167
Boalsburg, PA 16827
814-237-7703

Northeast Sierra Club
PO Box 1311
Scranton, PA 18501
www.pennsylvania.sierraclub.org/northeastern/index.asp
NESierra@aol.com

Pocono Outdoor Club
RR #8, Box 8142A
Stroudsburg, PA 18360
570-620-2492

Susquehanna Appalachian Trail Club
PO Box 61001
Harrisburg, PA 17106-1001
www.libertynet.org/susqatc

Susquehanna Trailers Hiking Club
93 Cedarwood Drive
Laflin, PA 18702
570-655-4979

Susquehannock Trail Club
PO Box 643
Coudersport, PA 16914

Bibliography

Braun, D. D., and J. D. Inners. *Ricketts Glen State Park, Luzerne, Sullivan and Columbia Counties—The Rocks, the Glens, and the Falls.* 2d ed. Pennsylvania Geological Survey, 4th ser., Park Guide 13, 1998.

Brugler, Milton A. *Sullivan County, Pennsylvania "Endless Mountains": Recreation, Mines, Industries, Agriculture, Personalities.* Williamsport, Pa.: Grit Publishing Co., year unknown.

Clarke, Staley N. *The Romance of Old Barclay.* Towanda, Pa.: Towanda Printing Co., 1928.

Gertler, Edward. *Keystone Canoeing—A Guide to Canoeable Waters in Eastern Pennsylvania.* 3d ed. Silver Spring, Md.: Seneca Press, 1993.

Geyer, Alan R., and William H. Bolles. *Outstanding Scenic Geological Features of Pennsylvania.* Pennsylvania Geological Survey, EG 7, 1979.

Geyer, Alan R., and William H. Bolles. *Outstanding Scenic Geological Features of Pennsylvania, Part 2.* Pennsylvania Geological Survey, EG 7, 1987.

McFarland, J., L. H. D. Horace, and Robert B. McFarland. *Eagles Mere and the Sullivan Highlands.* Harrisburg, Pa.: J. Horace McFarland Co., Mount Pleasant Press, 1944.

Ostrander, Stephen J. *Great Natural Areas in Eastern Pennsylvania.* Mechanicsburg, Pa.: Stackpole Books, 1996.

Petrillo, F. Charles. *Ghost Towns of North Mountain—Ricketts, Mountain Springs and Stull.* Wilkes Barre, Pa.: Wyoming Historical and Geological Society, 1991.

Royer, Denise W. *Worlds End State Park, Sullivan County, Geologic Features of Interest.* Pennsylvania Geological Survey, Park Guide 12.

Singmaster, Elise. *Pennsylvania's Susquehanna.* Harrisburg, Pa.: J. Horace McFarland Co., Mount Pleasant Press, 1950.

Stranahan, Susan Q. *Susquehanna—River of Dreams.* Baltimore: Johns Hopkins University Press, 1993.

Taber, Thomas Townsend. *Ghost Lumber Towns of Central Pennsylvania—Laquin, Masten, Ricketts, Grays Run.* Williamsport, Pa.: Lycoming Printing Co., 1970.

Wiemann, Barbara L., gen. ed. *Pennsylvania Hiking Trails.* 12th ed. Cogan Station, Pa.: Keystone Trails Association, 1998.

Wyoming County Sesquicentennial Committee, Wyoming County Historical Society. *Wyoming County Sesquicentennial—A Look Back.* Tunkhannock, Pa.: Mulligan Printing, 1992.

 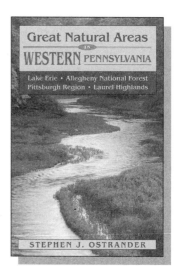